P9-CRI-040

THE ROLE OF INTERNATIONAL LAW
IN THE ELIMINATION OF WAR

THE ROLE OF

INTERNATIONAL LAW

IN THE

ELIMINATION OF WAR

by

QUINCY WRIGHT

Professor Emeritus of International Law
University of Chicago
Professor of Foreign Affairs
University of Virginia

MANCHESTER UNIVERSITY PRESS
U.S.A.: OCEANA PUBLICATIONS INC.
1961

© 1961 Manchester University Press
Published by the University of Manchester at
THE UNIVERSITY PRESS
316–324 Oxford Road, Manchester, 13

U.S.A.
OCEANA PUBLICATIONS INC.
80 Fourth Avenue, New York, 3, N.Y.
Library of Congress Catalog Card Number 61–18186

Printed in Great Britain by Butler & Tanner Ltd., Frome and London

CONTENTS

v

FOREWORD

By her Will, the late Miss Olive Schill of Prestbury, Cheshire, an old friend of the University, whose portrait is painted in Lady Katharine Chorley's *Manchester Made Them*, left the sum of £10,000 to the University in memory of her brother, Melland Schill, who died in the 1914–18 War. The annual income from this sum is to be used to promote and publish a series of public lectures of the highest possible standard dealing with International Law.

The following set of five lectures deals with the role of international law in the elimination of war and the settlement of international disputes.

Dr. Quincy Wright has spent a lifetime in the teaching and study of international law institutions and his lectures should be regarded as a valuable introduction to the law student and to the general reader on the most pressing problems of our age.

B. A. WORTLEY

Faculty of Law,
The University of Manchester
November, 1961

Chapter I

THE FUNCTIONS OF INTERNATIONAL LAW

THE role of international law can be approached from the points of view of the functions, the history, the conditions, and the content of that law. I plan to devote a lecture to each of these approaches, considering in my final lecture the potential and, I hope, future role of international law in the elimination of war and the settlement of international disputes.

1. ORDER AND JUSTICE

The functions of international law, as of any system of law, are to assist in the maintenance of order and in the administration of justice. These two functions are different and methods used to promote each may be inconsistent with methods to promote the other. Order may be maintained, as it is in primitive societies, by a body of precise prohibitions so incorporated in the culture, so easy to understand and apply, so maintained by custom and practice, that violation is rare, reparation is prompt if there is violation, and regular observance or reparation avoids the usual causes of irritation, retaliation, and violence. Prohibitions of murder, rape, adultery, assault, and theft are of this character. In pre-literate tribal societies, the appropriate response, whether of self-help or community action, is defined by custom.

In early literate societies, offences are defined in codes like those of Hammurabi (2100 B.C.), Rome (XII Tables, 450 B.C.), Manu (A.D. 100), and Ethelbert of Kent (A.D. 600). They emphasize objective facts rather than subjective attitudes. Offences are usually treated, not as crimes, but as torts defined by concrete injuries each with a designated reparation to be paid to the injured party. Order may also be maintained, as in empires and autocracies, by the central organization of power and administration preventing disorder by pervasive policing and enforcement of decrees by swift, certain, and severe punishment. Such systems of order, as Machiavelli pointed out, are

1

characteristic of a 'new prince' who, having won his throne by force and fraud, finds it difficult to rule by other methods. Modern totalitarian regimes have at first maintained order by such procedures but have tended to rely more on custom, consent, and 'due process of law' as they become older, sanctions characteristic of 'old princes' according to Machiavelli.[1]

The use of arbitrary prohibitions, pervasive policing, and severe punishment to maintain order give rise to complaints of gross injustice as peoples become more civilized and less intimidated. Such methods may be contrasted with the use of impartial adjudication, common law, legislation by representative bodies, and civil administration to maintain justice. Adjudication is exemplified in the early history of nations by provision of impartial and percipient tribunals enjoying the confidence of the litigants to examine and decide controversies according to established custom or the wisdom of experience, paying attention to intentions and justifications as well as to acts and injuries. Legislation appears when increasing public expenditures, usually for war, wider contacts and superior technology, breaking the 'cake of custom' and introducing the idea of 'progress', induce monarchs to summon representative bodies to provide revenue and declare or recommend principles, supplementing custom and reflecting the changing values and conditions of the society. Administrative agencies, staffed by a competent civil service, to facilitate co-operation among 'interest groups' and to implement public policies of economic and social welfare, develop as simple agriculture is supplemented by trade and industry, as cities develop, as a literate middle class emerges, and as social relationships become increasingly complex.

These processes of justice may exist without the support of a central power superior to that of the litigants, as in the institutions of pacific settlement, peaceful change, and social and economic co-operation of the League of Nations and the United Nations, but in this case they cannot assure justice when their prescriptions conflict with the national interests of powerful states. 'Justice without force is powerless, force without justice is tyrannical,' observed Pascal.[2] He, therefore, recommended a yoking of force and justice through law. History suggests that in proportion as conditions change rapidly, satisfactory societies require institutions with the capability both to determine what is right and to exert the might to enforce it. But

---

[1] Niccolo Machiavelli, *The Prince*, chaps. 2, 3, 6.
[2] Blaise Pascal, *Les Pensées*, Paris, 1877, vol. 1, p. 100.

history also suggests that the coexistence of these capabilities implies a considerable consensus on values among the members of the society, including the value of maintaining the society itself.[1]

But while the coexistence and mutual support of prohibitions, police, adjudication, legislation, and administration are to be found in most advanced societies, the emphasis on each differs in degree, and it appears that in the history of societies these characteristics do not, apart from outside influences, appear simultaneously, but in the order stated.

Consider as an example England, a state which developed in comparative isolation through many centuries. This society, though its roots go back to Roman and Anglo-Saxon times, did not become a political society until William the Conqueror organized sufficient power to maintain peace throughout the land, utilizing the prohibitions of custom observed by the people. Within that peace there grew, after a century, a judicial system able to settle controversies in accordance with law. Not until the common law had developed for another century was Parliament established with legislative authority. Centuries later, central administrative authorities other than the King's Courts were established to collect taxes, to maintain a national army and navy, and to administer economic and social policies. First, strict law prohibiting breaches of order, then executive and military power to keep the peace, then courts to administer justice and settle controversies, then a legislative body to modify the common law and declare public policy, and, finally, a centralized administration to direct the realization of that policy—this was the historical process by which the English government developed.

It must not be thought that this sequence was absolute or that it proceeded smoothly and without interruption. William the Conqueror could not have maintained an executive authority able to maintain peace unless the Anglo-Saxon kingdoms had developed much strict law, and even then Norman power was unable to prevent anarchy in the reign of Stephen and Matilda. Henry II could hardly have established the King's Courts with obligatory jurisdiction under the possessory assizes if rudimentary ideas of the common law had not existed as well as the king's executive power. The Model Parliament of Edward I had antecedents in the Curia Regis, which went

[1] Percy E. Corbett, *Law in Diplomacy*, Princeton University Press, 1959, p. 275; Quincy Wright, *A Study of War*, University of Chicago Press, 1942, p. 835; *The Strengthening of International Law*, The Hague, Academy of International Law, Recueil des Cours, 1959, pp. 12 ff.

back to Anglo-Saxon times, and the great administrative departments, developed by the Tudors, had behind them certain officials and commissions which had performed administrative functions in early Norman times. Furthermore, there were lapses of central power during the reign of John in the thirteenth century, during that of Edward II in the fourteenth, and during the War of the Roses in the fifteenth, and the evolution of the power of Parliament was spasmodic.

Nevertheless, it appears that in the development of political society great advances in adjudication can hardly be expected until the peace is assured and some common custom exists; nor are great advances in legislation and administration likely until adjudication has developed a common law. Yet some attention must be given to each of these aspects of government from the first. Executive power which seeks to enforce peace without law is likely to prove a short-lived tyranny, and courts to enforce law cannot function satisfactorily in a dynamic society unless there is a legislature or other organ with capacity to supplement and modify the law as new conditions arise. Legislation as well as adjudication implies administration. Obviously no aspect of government can exist without some development of all the others, but history suggests a natural order in each stage of which a particular aspect deserves primary attention.

The United Nations has rudiments of all these processes of government. The Charter prohibits the use or threat of force, and the Security Council is authorized to keep the peace. The International Court is available to administer justice; the General Assembly and the conferences of the Specialized Agencies are available to engage in quasi-legislation; and the Economic and Social Council, the Trusteeship Council, the Secretariat, and the Governing Bodies and Secretariats of the Specialized Agencies are prepared to administer policy. Each supplements the others to build a world political society, but it seems doubtful whether any will be able to function satisfactorily until the prohibition of aggression is clarified, and the organs for preventing aggression have the capacity to act and sufficient power to maintain international peace and security. If the members of the United Nations prove unwilling or unable to accomplish this purpose, put first in the Charter, by voluntary action, yielding some of their sovereignty, it may be accomplished by the conqueror's sword after another war over such remnants of humanity as survive. The establishment of 'universal states' by this method has, according to Arnold Toynbee, been the usual course of civilizations following the time of troubles and the bi-polarization of the balance of power.[1] The 'organization' of peace following its 'proclamation', said Prime Minister Aristide Briand on signing in 1928 the pact which bears his name, 'is the first step in building a universal community in the shrunken world'.[2] 'The absolute primacy that the theorists assign to the jurisdictional function artificially inverts the terms of the problem,' writes Charles De Visscher, former president of the International Court of Justice. 'So long as the individualistic distribution of power among states persists, with the major political tensions that it engenders, peace will serve justice better than justice will serve peace.'[3]

Second only to the maintenance of order, referred to by M. Briand as 'the work of tomorrow', is the organization of justice—the establishment of procedures for settling disputes not only peacefully but also justly, through the development of international law and courts to administer it. The attainment of a representative world legislature able to make new laws, and of central agencies with authoritative powers to administer them, must await greater evolution of world culture and a greater spirit of co-operation. For some time international legislation will, no doubt, be limited to the process of treaty-making, supplemented by interpretations and recommendations in resolutions of international conferences such as the General Assembly of the United Nations.[4] International administration, apart from the administration of their own offices and staff by international agencies, will depend in large measure upon voluntary co-operation of national governments in implementing the proposals of international bodies in their territories.[5]

Thus both history and analysis suggest that order must come before justice. The latter is a delicate plant that cannot thrive in a

[1] Arnold F. Toynbee, *A Study of History*, vol. 3, pp. 145 ff., vol. 6, pp. 315 ff.; Wright, *A Study of War*, pp. 117, 128, 382, 690, 763; 'Empires and World Governments before 1918', *Current History*, August, 1960, vol. 39, pp. 65 ff.

[2] Address August 27, 1928, in U.S. Department of State, *Treaty for the Renunciation of War*, 1933, p. 315.

[3] Charles De Visscher, *Theory and Reality in Public International Law*, Princeton University Press, 1957, p. 328. See below, p. 6, n. 1.

[4] The Commission to Study the Organization of Peace proposed legislation by concurrent action of the General Assembly and the Security Council in limited fields outside the territory of any state (11th Report, *Organizing Peace in the Nuclear Age*, 1959; 13th Report, *Developing the United Nations*, 1961, A. N. Holcombe, ed. See also Wright, *The Strengthening of International Law*, above p. 3, n. 1, pp. 127 ff.).

[5] Wright, 'Some Administrative Problems of International Law', *Indian Journal of Public Administration*, 1959, vol. 5, pp. 371 ff.

climate of fear and violence. Without order, the strong will seek to obtain their own brand of justice by self-help, denying justice to the weak, promoting disorder, and disrupting society.[1]

[1] An argument to the contrary has been elaborated by Julius Stone, who writes: 'As Sir Gerald Fitzmaurice (the legal adviser to the British Foreign Office) and others have pointed out, the enthusiastic efforts to ban all uses of force in relations between states, except in defence of one's own territory against armed attack, have had the ironic effect of weakening international law. Formerly, when the use of force in support of legal rights was regarded as licensed, small powers favoured third-party settlement because equality before the law was better than inequality on the battlefield. But when atomic weapons are obviously too formidable to use in vindicating most kinds of legal rights; and when the opposed military bloc threatens nuclear retaliation against pressure exerted by conventional forces (as the Soviet Union did in the Suez and Cuban crises), then plausibility is given to the notion that force is out of the question even for the defence of legal rights. When it begins to appear that small states can violate with impunity the rights of big states, the interest of the small ones in third-party settlement understandably diminishes. In so far as a blanket prohibition is now assumed to be placed on the use of force by any state, even to enforce its legal rights, the effect is to undermine the modest binding power which international law enjoyed in the old-fashioned days before the League of Nations and the United Nations.' (*Foreign Affairs*, July, 1961, vol. 39, p. 553.) Stone elaborates this argument in his book *Aggression and World Order*, London, 1958. This argument seems to assume that great states will always observe the rights of small states and use their superior power only to enforce their rights against such states, but that small states are inclined to violate the rights of others if they can. This assumption raises an issue of fact: whether the enforcement of rights was the usual motivation of the great European powers in their frequent uses of force against small states, especially those of Asia and Africa during the nineteenth century; and also an issue of law concerning the source of the rights asserted by those powers. It may be that the hesitancy of Asian, African, and Communist states to accept third-party adjudication in recent times arises from fear that this process might support claims, founded on superior force, which they consider unjust. This was suggested in a debate in the American Society of International Law in 1953 (*Proceedings*, pp. 48–89), introduced by Oliver Lissitzyn with the remark: 'International law is a heritage of the Christian West. In the age of expansion of Europe it was largely imposed on the rest of the world. More often this was a matter of Western self-interest rather than a matter of Christian morality. . . . Can a body of principles and precedents so exclusively Western in origin be successfully transmuted into a world law which is freely accepted by nations of widely different historical backgrounds?' The Ambassador from Indonesia, an attaché of the Saudi Arabian embassy and an expert on Soviet Russia, read papers followed by extensive comment inducing the present writer to remark: 'In all stages of international law we seem to have had those two principles—the principle of imperialism and the principle of reciprocity. States that have the power are always inclined to take what they can get and to use international law to justify what they have obtained. That is the principle of international law to which the Soviets have given great emphasis, especially in relations with the smaller states that surrounded them. Among equals, however, they sometimes acknowledge another principle of international law based on reciprocity. Now the question is, which will prevail?' (p. 80; see also below, p. 11, n. 1; p. 16, n. 1).

2. The Meaning of Order

Order implies a measure of predictability of cultural, social, economic, and political relations making it possible for members of a society to plan their futures. Social order is to politics what the order of nature is to science. Without confidence in the order of nature as observed in the past, scientists cannot develop formulae for prediction, or technologies for control, of natural phenomena. Without confidence in a modicum of social order, neither governments nor people can plan for justice or reform. If all is flux, human reason is stymied and human will is paralysed.

Predictability implies a measure of stability in cultural, social, economic, and political institutions. Institutions such as states, churches, universities, business corporations, and international organizations are combinations of customs, values, doctrines, and authorities. Because the influence which institutions have exerted on the behaviour and decisions of individuals and groups in the past can be anticipated in the future, social affairs become in a measure predictable. However, social scientists and social operators can make predictions only on the assumption that the major social institutions will continue or will change only gradually.[1]

Institutional change, however, is inevitable in a world of continuous scientific discovery, technological invention, and propagation of new ideas and values. Institutions must continually adapt themselves to the new conditions which arise from these circumstances or they will encourage revolt and violence, promoting instability. But if institutional change proceeds at a rate beyond the threshold of psychic adaptation, it becomes revolution, not evolution, and also encourages violence, destroying stability.

[1] The social sciences rest on human psychology, but man is a social animal (Aristotle). He lives in a world of symbols (Cassirer) and institutions. Individual psychology, except perhaps in the case of very young children, cannot be studied apart from social conditioning. Hobbes' distinction between man in a 'state of nature' and man in a 'state of society' is an abstraction of limited applicability, as indicated by the tendency of philosophies of anarchy and communism to converge. Institutions exist both in social systems and in individual minds. Groups and their members continually interact; consequently, sociology and psychology are two approaches to the same problem, that of human behaviour. See my Kelsen Lectures, 1952, on the 'Institutionalizing of International Peace and Security', *Problems of Stability and Progress in International Relations* (University of California Press, 1954, pp. 3 ff.), and my analysis of sociology and psychology in *The Study of International Relations*, New York, Appleton-Century-Crofts, 1955, pp. 390, 415.

The sources of instability are, therefore, excessive institutional rigidity or fluidity when faced by changing conditions, material or ideological. While among primitive peoples natural disasters— famine, flood, epidemics, overpopulation, soil erosion, and climatic change—have been major sources of social change, among civilized peoples human action—scientific discovery, technological inventions, ideological propaganda, and war—has been of greater importance.[1] In modern civilization, war, utilizing means of great destruction, has created conditions often frustrating institutional adaptation. It has become the great source of sudden change and instability, and the great barrier to social prediction.[2] Among historic civilizations it has sometimes brought progress, but more often retrogression. States and civilizations have been built by war but also destroyed by war. The probability of such destruction is greater in the future because of the overwhelming capabilities of nuclear weapons, initiating a wholly new order in the history of warfare.[3]

It is true that in the past societies have often sought stability by suppressing science, technology, and novel ideas and values, rather than by suppressing violence. But the contemporary world is committed to progress in human welfare, dependent upon such changes. Institutions must seek to adapt themselves to these elements of progress, a task not impossible for modern institutions, less bound by custom than were their forebears.[4] It seems on the other hand unlikely that they can adapt themselves to the extreme destruction which would result from nuclear war, though some advocates of the science of deterrence think they can,[5] without considering the influence of preparations to this end in precipitating such a war.[6] International order is, therefore, in large measure synonymous with the abolition of war, and rules of order are mainly concerned with the control of war. This in fact has been the main concern of both international law and the United Nations.

[1] I have classified these under the heads Catastrophe, Corruption, Conversion, and Conquest in *A Study of War*, p. 393. See also pp. 202 ff.

[2] All generals affirm that 'the outcome of an encounter cannot be predicted and has no appearance of being predetermined, but arises, in the likeness of a new creation, out of the encounter itself'. Toynbee, *op. cit.*, vol. 1, p. 301; Wright, *A Study of War*, p. 128.

[3] *Ibid.*, pp. 130, 256, 272, 378, 397.

[4] *Ibid.*, pp. 402 ff.; Wright, *Problems of Stability and Progress*, pp. 11 ff.

[5] See Herman Kahn, *On Thermo-Nuclear War*, Princeton University Press, 1960.

[6] Wright, *A Study of War*, p. 1223.

3. The Meaning of Justice

Justice implies that the outcome of disputes or conflicts shall be in a measure satisfactory to the society and even to the litigants. It is perhaps uncommon for the loser in a litigation to be happy about it, but in a well-ordered society with established standards of justice, he is usually ready to accept the judgment.

Disputes and conflicts are the consequence of the coexistence of self-determining individuals and societies, called by sociologists 'systems of action'.[1] They become more frequent as such systems of action become more numerous and closer together, through abundant communication and trade, developing interdependencies—economic, social, political, and cultural. They may be dealt with by arbitrary authority equipped with power and devoted to the maintenance of order without consideration of justice. But how can they be settled justly? Some positivistic jurists deny that justice can be objectively defined.

Each system of action, they say, defines justice according to its internal characteristics and its particular situation. These divergent conceptions of justice cause disputes and conflicts incapable of settlement except through the application of positive law. Thus objective justice distinct from positive law is an illusion.[2] If negotiation by the parties fails to achieve a settlement by compromise or bargain, and if neither party is capable of dictating to the other, settlement is possible only if both submit to a superior authority. They are not likely to do so unless that authority is bound to apply positive rules of a legal order which binds them both.

Thomas Hobbes assumed that the situation of man in the 'state of nature', in which there was no positive law, was a war of all against all—*bellum omnium contra omnes*. He could conceive of no common values or principles of justice in such a situation. Each man was interested only in his own self-preservation, and only if the inconvenience of this situation so influenced human reason that all joined in a social contract giving up their natural liberty to an absolute sovereignty was peace possible, and only in that case could

[1] Talcott Parsons and Edward Shils, eds., *Toward a General Theory of Action*, Cambridge, Harvard University Press, 1951.

[2] Hans Kelsen, *What Is Justice?* University of California Press, 1957: 'I cannot say what justice is, this absolute justice for which mankind is longing. I must acquiesce in a relative justice and I can only say what justice is to me.' (P. 24; see also p. 173.) See my review, *American Journal of International Law*, October, 1957, vol. 51, p. 830.

a brand of justice identified with the will of the sovereign be administered.[1]

In the society of nations there is some support for this concept, as, indeed, Hobbes suggested. Each nation has its own culture, its own values, its own procedures which its own people consider just. Each finds it difficult to envisage a universal justice except as an extension of its own conceptions. There are, therefore, few universally accepted standards of ethics or justice beyond those manifested in the sources of international law. Sovereignty implies self-determination of justice. It is the manifestation of that arrogance, or *hubris*, discussed by Greek philosophers, in contrast to *themis*, which recognized the principle of reciprocity. This 'natural law' assumed a higher justice capable of adjudicating between the subjective standards of each litigant.[2]

It is doubtless true that justice is a function of a community in which men communicate, of a culture emerging from their exchange of ideas and values, and of a society in which co-operation toward some goals, flowing from these common values, develops. Such a community, culture, and society may exist in varying degrees without the organization of government or of central compulsion. The germs of universal justice were to be found in the contacts established among all human civilizations at the time of the discoveries. These germs have developed with the printing press, steam navigation, telecommunications, the aeroplane, and other devices augmenting the abundance of economic, social, and cultural interchange, and inducing the establishment of international organizations to promote co-operation in the fields of communication, trade, health, education, science, labour standards, peaceful use of atomic energy, and many other subjects of common interest.

Universal principles of justice, therefore, exist in embryo, and some of them have been asserted in the United Nations Charter by such terms as self-determination, human rights, sovereign equality, and social and economic welfare, as well as in principles of general international law concerning treatment of aliens, reparation for injuries, observance of agreements, and mutual respect for territory and independence.

The administration of justice, however, involves not only the

---

[1] Hobbes, *Leviathan*, chap. 15.
[2] This does not, of course, assert an 'absolute' justice, but only a relative justice higher than that of the litigants and capable of solving their dispute (above p. 9, n. 2).

declaration of generally accepted principles, but also sufficient elaboration to indicate their application in concrete situations, and the establishment of tribunals and procedures assuring such application if conflicting parties fail to agree. Justice requires third-party adjudication, instead of self-help, if negotiation, either direct or assisted by the processes of mediation, conciliation, inquiry, consultation, or conference, fails to achieve agreement satisfactory to the parties and not unsatisfactory to others or the community as a whole.

Such adjudication may take the form of arbitration in which emphasis is on the confidence of the parties in the tribunal which they have selected by special agreement, or of judicial settlement in which emphasis is on the confidence of the parties in the law which the tribunal is bound to apply. The first procedure—adjudication by 'good men'—is said to have been favoured by the Confucian philosophy and to have been characteristic of China until recent times.[1] The latter procedure—justice according to law—has been characteristic of the West. Both have figured in international litigation but there has been great reluctance by states to assume positive obligations to submit to either procedure. The great differences in ideology make it difficult to find an arbitrator in whom both sides will have confidence. Premier Nikita Khrushchev, generalizing from his disappointment in the Congo situation of 1960, said that neutral states might be possible but not neutral men; and Maxim Litvinoff once said: 'Only an angel could be unbiased in judging Russian affairs.'[2]

The differences in civilizations also raise doubts, especially in the new states of Asia and Africa, not to mention the Communist states, whether international law stemming from the Greek philosophy, Roman law, and Christian ethics of the West reflects standards of justice consonant with their own philosophies or religions.[3] It appears possible that studies of comparative law, documenting Western maxims of justice from the great books of the East, might moderate these doubts.

---

[1] J. Escarra, *Le Régime des concessions étrangères en Chine*, The Hague, Academy of International Law, Recueil des Cours, 1929, vol. 27 (II); F. S. C. Northrop, *The Meeting of East and West*, New York, 1946; Wright, *Legal Problems in the Far Eastern Conflict*, Institute of Pacific Relations, 1941, pp. 8 ff.; 'Asian Experience and International Law', *International Studies* (Quarterly Journal of the Indian School of International Studies), July, 1959, vol. 1, p. 80; *The Strengthening of International Law*, pp. 68 ff.

[2] Netherlands Department of Foreign Affairs, *Conference at The Hague on Russian Affairs*, 1922, p. 126; Louis B. Sohn, *Cases and Other Materials on World Law*, Brooklyn, Foundation Press, 1950, p. 1046.

[3] Above n. 1.

At the present time, however, it appears that the processes of contact, communication, acculturation, and co-operation have not proceeded to the point where principles of justice or procedures of adjudication will be so widely accepted that third-party settlement of all international disputes not settled by agreement of the parties can be assured. Furthermore, it does not seem likely that this will occur until a system of order is sufficiently established to make reliance upon self-help for physical security unnecessary. The states will continue to regard their national interest in self-preservation superior to observance of justice, and so long as that security depends on power position, they will not risk submission to impartial adjudication which might jeopardize that position. The United States, which more than most states has professed an allegiance to international law and the principle of international adjudication, has, up to date, insisted upon a self-judging reservation to its acceptance of the optional clause of the Statute of the International Court of Justice.[1]

4. COMPARISON OF RULES OF ORDER AND JUSTICE

Order and justice are clearly related. Justice cannot be administered unless there is a modicum of order. It seems unlikely that order can be permanently maintained if justice is ignored. The two, however, are not identical and it appears that historically order must precede justice. The first problem of the modern community of nations is to establish greater confidence than now exists in an order which abolishes war.

Law can have an important function in both the maintenance of order and the administration of justice. It is true that both may get along without law. Order may for a time be maintained by brute force behind decrees or orders of the supreme authority with so little generality of application that they hardly deserve the name of law. But in a large society, where the maintenance of order requires a considerable service, civilian or military, convenience requires that decrees have sufficient generality and permanence to make them law. Furthermore, expediency suggests, even to the most ruthless dictator, that decrees appeal in some degree to the sense of justice of those to whom they are addressed, moderating their disposition to resist.

[1] A proposal to repeal this Connally reservation was before the Senate Foreign Relations Committee in 1961.

Requirements of clarity, convenience, and expediency tend toward order through law apart from belief in justice.[1]

It is also true that justice may be administered without law. The practice of arbitration by a person expert not in law but in the trade involved in the litigation, or by a 'good man' respected by the litigants for his wisdom and sense of justice, rather than his knowledge of law, is well known, and induces some to insist on the superiority of justice without law.[2] However, in complex societies the rule of law is generally accepted. Even Oriental societies which in some cases have had a traditional predisposition toward informal arbitration or conciliation[3] have generally accepted codes of European origin since coming in contact with the West and now administer justice with law, although their interpretations of a code, in consideration of local customs and standards, are frequently different from those of the country of its origin.

Justice and order are related, but law aiming primarily at order is different from that aiming primarily at justice.

To maintain order, whether sanctioned by custom or by central power, law should be expressed in rules which are so clear and precise that he who runs may read. They must be like the rules of the road which direct the driver to turn to the right or to the left, to stop at a red light and proceed on a green; or like the possessory assizes of King Henry II, which forbade self-help and required submission to the King's Court in certain clearly defined situations of rival claims to land. These assizes were rules of order to prevent violence and were sharply distinguished from the merits of the dispute to be later decided in the King's Courts according to the common law embodying principles of justice.

Sir John Fischer Williams elaborated this comparison of the requirements of order in medieval England with those of international relations after World War I as follows:

The wrongdoer who had a tortious seisin had, nevertheless, as a result of the higher duty of preserving peace, the right of legal protection under that statute which, we are told, had cost our Henry II some sleepless nights— the Assize of Novel Disseisin; the king had to discourage self-help, and he based his law on the paramount importance of peace. . . . The Covenant of the League of Nations, with its Article 10, seeks to give international

---

[1] Machiavelli, though emphasizing power, recognized these conditions.

[2] Roscoe Pound, 'Justice According to Law', *Columbia Law Review*, 1931, vol. 13, pp. 696 ff.; 1914, vol. 14, pp. 1 ff., pp. 103 ff.

[3] Above p. 11, n. 1.

society that stability of possession which Henry II sought to give to twelfth-century England.[1]

Sir John noted that the League was less perfect in not providing a 'writ of right' ultimately to determine the better right superseding the possessory title initially protected, but did not question the wisdom of the League in establishing rules to preserve the peace even though states were not ready to submit to an administration of justice by third-party adjudication.

Among the rules of order in international law are those forbidding the threat or use of force, limiting self-defence, authorizing collective-security action, and defining diplomatic immunities. So long as the basic principle of international order is mutual respect for the territorial integrity and political independence of states, order can hardly be expected unless states and the United Nations are provided with clear rules defining what constitutes lack of such respect. Definitions of aggression and self-defence, resting as far as possible on easily observable facts rather than on motives or attitudes, are, therefore, of major importance, especially in view of the difficulty of decision in the Security Council and the General Assembly. Discretion on these matters should be reduced to the minimum.

It is true that the Charter intended to give a considerable discretion to the Security Council to decide such issues on the basis of the facts of a situation; and on some questions, such as what constitutes a threat to use armed force or a threat to the peace, discretion is necessary. Experience, however, underlines the need for definitions as precise as possible of what constitutes, for example, aggression, so that states will not commit it through inadvertence or through ignorance of what aggression is, as may have been the case in the Suez (1956) and Cuban (April, 1961) incidents. United Nations organs should not be able to evade their responsibility if a transgression occurs, though the question of what action is most expedient, faced in the Hungarian and Congo crises, requires the exercise of wise discretion. Those who have sought to make the term aggression identical with injustice have misconceived the function of the term in the Charter and in international law. It is a rule of order, not of justice.[2]

For the adjudication of disputes, a different kind of law is neces-

---

[1] 'Sovereignty, Seisin and the League', *British Year Book of International Law*, 1926, pp. 35 ff.
[2] See Julius Stone, *Aggression and World Order*, 1958.

sary, less positive and more equitable. Justice requires a flexible adaptation of decisions to all the facts of the case and to the interests of all the litigants as well as to the principles of society as a whole. Over-precise rules of law militate against that flexibility. *Summa jus summa injuria.* General principles, stating presumptions which may be overridden by special circumstances, maxims of justice, and principles of 'natural law' appealing to the values of the community and the litigants, are useful. Their function is both to guide the judge and to appeal to his audience. *Pacta sunt servanda. Rebus sic stantibus. Jus ex injuria non oritur. Ex factis jus oritur. Sic utere tuo ut alienum non laedas.* These are familiar maxims which are useful even though they may in some circumstances conflict with each other, and even though their application in particular circumstances may require long discussion and considerable discretionary judgment.

A negotiator or a court attempting to determine justice in a dispute is not faced by the exigency inevitable in a problem of maintaining order but has ample time to assemble facts and listen to all sides of the argument, to deliberate, to weigh, and to judge. The United Nations Charter and general international law include, as has been noted, principles of justice as well as rules of order. Some of these principles may be regarded as more political than juridical. It is difficult to see how a court could determine whether a people is entitled to self-determination, or what should be done to promote social and economic welfare of different peoples. These are problems for political judgment. However, whether the body applying them is a tribunal or a political body, these principles suggest broad lines of progress toward values cherished by the Community of Nations.

The difference between these two types of rules was recognized by the League of Nations and the United Nations in their insistence that the function of the international organization in preventing illegal resort to force is distinct from, and prior to, consideration of the merits of a particular controversy which threatens the peace. As pointed out, this principle is the same as that which figured in Henry II's possessory assizes. It has been realized by statesmen in imperfect legal communities that the mixing of the two—a common device of powerful potential aggressors—renders the preservation of order impossible. The immediate action necessary to preserve the peace and to prevent violence cannot be delayed by debate on whether the state threatening violence has real grievances. If such debate is permitted, the aggressor will have completed his conquest before action is taken, as did Japan in Manchuria. The original injustice complained of by the aggressor will have been compounded by new injustices to the victim. Both order and justice will have been sacrificed. Nothing seems more important to the present situation of the world than reaffirmation of this distinction by the formulation of precise rules of international order prohibiting violence, and procedures for applying them, distinct from procedures for determining fundamental justice in disputes.

The International Court of Justice gave clear expression to this position in the Corfu Channel Case, when it unanimously condemned the British mine-sweeping operations in the Corfu Channel three weeks after the explosion of October 22, 1946, which had damaged British warships in innocent passage, killing personnel—an explosion for which it found Albania responsible. The British alleged that the mine-sweeping operation was an exercise of the 'right of intervention' and of 'self-help' in the interest of justice, but the Court considered it

'the manifestation of a policy of force, such as has, in the past, given rise to most serious abuses and such as cannot, whatever be the present defects in international organization, find a place in international law. . . . From the nature of things, it would be reserved for the most powerful states and might easily lead to perverting the administration of international justice itself . . . Between independent States, respect for territorial sovereignty is an essential foundation of international relations. The Court recognizes that the Albanian Government's complete failure to carry out its duties after the explosions, and the dilatory nature of its diplomatic notes, are extenuating circumstances for the action of the United Kingdom Government. But to ensure respect for international law, of which it is the organ, the Court must declare that the action of the British Navy constituted a violation of Albanian sovereignty.[1]

In my next lecture, I will discuss the interplay of these two functions of law in the history of international law.

[1] 'The Corfu Channel Case (Merits)', *I.C.J. Reports*, 1949, p. 4; *American Journal of International Law*, July, 1949, vol. 43, pp. 582, 583; see also above p. 6, n. 1.

Chapter II

THE HISTORY OF INTERNATIONAL LAW

1. Underlying Conditions and Legal Change

The history of international law discloses the interplay of the two functions of that law, on the one hand of maintaining order and on the other of administering justice in the society of nations. Both functions have been influenced by conditions of technology and ideology.

In the European Middle Ages, for example, technical conditions so limited military communication, transport, and attack that feudal castles were relatively invulnerable and central authority could not preserve order among predatory barons by material means. Medieval monarchs sought to establish rules of order, such as the possessory assizes of Henry II, but the difficulty of doing so, under the conditions of the time, was illustrated by the struggles of Henry's son John with both the barons below and the Pope above. Such difficulties were recurrent in England and typical of secular authority under similar conditions not only in Europe but in the Middle East and India.

On the other hand, a common ideology, propagated throughout Christendom by the clergy, gave support to basic principles of justice. Under these conditions supra-national law devoted itself to abstract conceptions concerning the justice of war, which, supported by the spiritual sanctions of the Church, had a certain influence.

Contrasted with this, the technological developments since the Renaissance, particularly during the nineteenth century, made it possible for national states to maintain internal order, for European states with superior military technology to maintain order in overseas empires, and for a relatively stable balance of power, supported by British policy, the British Navy, and British finance, to provide material sanctions for international order. On the other hand, the many diverse nationalities, each demanding sovereignty, and the absence of a universal religion, militated against general acceptance of ideas of justice. International law, under these conditions,

17

emphasized positive rules to assist in the maintenance of order, by regulating war and stabilizing the balance of power, with little attention to principles of justice or natural law.

In the most recent period, new techniques, augmenting the destructiveness of war and making all states vulnerable to attack, have resulted in efforts to establish more comprehensive rules of order by outlawing war altogether through collective security action. At the same time the abundance of communications and the shrinking of the world, with the initial effect of multiplying and augmenting controversies among states of different nationality and ideology, have hampered this effort and directed more attention to principles of justice to facilitate peaceful settlement of disputes. The United Nations, like the League of Nations before it, has the joint function of preventing war and promoting peaceful settlement of disputes. Both institutions, however, have given priority to the first function. States have been prepared to assume positive obligations to refrain from use or threat of force and in principle to submit to the coercive sanctions of international organizations to maintain this rule, but they have not been willing to submit to other than voluntary procedures for the just settlement of their controversies. Despite this difference, it is generally recognized that international law, today, must provide both rules of order and principles of justice to facilitate these two processes. Let us consider in more detail the history of international law.

2. ANCIENT AND MEDIEVAL INTERNATIONAL LAW

Rules of international law have always developed when a number of independent states, whether tribal, city, imperial, feudal, or national, have been in continuous relations—commercial, cultural, or military—with one another. Such contacts have led to communication, to the comparison of values, to the discovery of common principles or interests, to the initiation of co-operation toward common goals, and eventually to the creation of institutions, organizations, and laws to maintain order and justice among the related states.

International law existed during certain periods in the history of ancient Egypt, Mesopotamia, Palestine, India, China, Greece, and Rome, though such periods were usually preceded by periods of political disintegration and chaos and followed by periods of political integration and widespread empire. In none of these periods was international law developed into a coherent system. It existed in general precepts of morality or religion, and in isolated customs and conventions imperfectly distinguishing foreign policies from legal rights, moral duties from legal obligations, or rules of order from principles of justice. The latter distinction was recognized in the Roman terms Lex and Jus, reflected to some extent in international relations in the distinction between Lex Fetiale, a body of formal rules applied by the Fetial College to determine the propriety of war or peace, and the Jus Gentium, which referred, however, not to the law between nations but to the law applied by the Praetor Peregrinus in administering justice in disputes between individuals of different nations.[1]

Modern international law developed on the break-up of European Christendom in the fifteenth century. Medieval Christendom, which had combined Christian ethics with the traditions of Imperial Rome and the philosophy of Greece, conceived itself as a universal community, governed spiritually by the Pope and temporally by the Holy Roman Emperor. It had united to fight the infidel in the Crusades from the eleventh to the fourteenth centuries and had sought to moderate local fighting, not only by the sentiment of loyalty to Christianity, but also by the Peace of God, declared by the ecclesiastical synods in the tenth century, prohibiting war in sacred localities and against the clergy, women, and peasants; and by the Truce of God, proclaimed soon after, prohibiting war on Holy Days. These rules of order were distinct from the principles of justice which medieval theologians and jurists developed from Greek and Roman conceptions of the law of nature. According to these principles civil law should be subordinate and supplementary to the universal law of nature which recognized the equality of man, the sanctity of agreements, and the impropriety of war unless properly declared, by adequate authority, with just causes, good motives, and reasonable expectations of promoting justice. St. Augustine, in the fourth century A.D., alarmed by the attacks of heathen barbarians on the Christian Roman Empire, abandoned the pacifism of the Sermon on the Mount and early Christianity and adopted the principle of 'Just War'. This theory was supported by Isidore of Seville (633), Thomas Aquinas (1265), and other medieval theologians, and is still the official doctrine of the Catholic Church. Its basic principle, that war is just only if its general purpose and probable result are to promote justice, is hardly

[1] Quincy Wright, *A Study of War*, University of Chicago Press, 1942, pp. 152 ff.

a rule of order since its application requires an examination of what justice requires in the situation.[1]

This theoretical international law, derived from reason, was affected by changing conditions in the late Middle Ages. The failure of the Crusades weakened confidence in the eventual achievement of universality by the Christian community and in the general applicability of standards to determine which side was 'just' in war. The Crusades also introduced concepts of humanity and good faith even between enemies, discovered by Christian knights in the behaviour of the somewhat more civilized Saracens. The rise of maritime commerce led to codifications of sea law applicable in times both of peace and of war and contributed concepts of neutral rights at sea in the interest of the merchants and navigators. More important, however, was the influence of secular princes, utilizing the newly invented art of printing to propagate national loyalty in vernacular languages, and the newly invented gunpowder to subdue feudal castles within the realm and to liberate themselves from imperial and papal claims outside. The princes developed concepts of equal territorial sovereignty and 'Reason of State' as sufficient justification for war; practices of diplomatic intercourse and rules of diplomatic immunity; and rules for the conduct of war. These concepts, practices, and rules, especially among Italian princes, induced Niccolò Machiavelli (1511) to rationalize might as the source of right in international relations, thus initiating a new 'realism', breaking away from the medieval concept of natural law and relegating whatever rules of international relations remained to the category of rules of order rather than that of principles of justice.[2]

These tendencies toward territorial sovereignty in both theory and practice were further supported by the voyages to America, India, and China by European navigators, revealing to Europe the smallness of the medieval world, the varieties of civilization in the actual world, and the possibility of exploiting that world by war and trade.

3. THE 'CLASSICAL' PERIOD

Modern international law arose in response to these conditions. It was formulated by ecclesiastical jurists like Francis of Victoria

---

[1] Quincy Wright, *A Study of War*, pp. 158 ff.; C. J. Cadoux, *The Early Christian Attitude Toward War*, London, 1919; Luigi Sturzo, *The International Community and the Right of War*, New York, 1920; John Eppstein, *The Catholic Tradition of the Law of Nations*, Washington, 1935.

[2] Wright, *op. cit.*, pp. 166 ff., 598 ff.

(1532), who sought to define the relations of European states and the newly discovered states of America and Asia in terms of natural law, which assumed their jural equality irrespective of religion or power. Practice, however, following Machiavelli, regarded the New World as *Terra Nullius*, open to discovery, occupation, and colonization by European states. The secularizing influence of the Renaissance, reviving Europe's knowledge of ancient Greece and Rome, and the disruptive influence of the Reformation, destroying the unity of Christendom, further established the territorial sovereignty of the princes ruling by virtue of military, political, and administrative power.

The destructive Thirty Years War gave the final blow to the medieval concept of Christendom. In the Peace of Westphalia (1648), ending that war, Europe decided that religion should be kept out of international politics and that each prince should decide the religion of his people as a domestic question—*cuius regio, eius religio*. The secular prince was, therefore, in international law above religion.

During this transitional period the development of international law owed a great deal to certain writers designated 'classical', who, however, were divided into two schools. The 'naturalists' like Victoria (1532), Suarez (1612), Pufendorff (1672), Wolff (1749), and Vattel (1758) sought principles of justice in natural law, while the 'positivists' such as Ayala (1582), Gentili (1598), Zouche (1650), Rachel (1676), Textor (1680), Bynkershoek (1737), Moser (1780), and Martens (1787), paid greater attention to rules of order observed in practice. Hugo Grotius (1625), whose great work on War and Peace appeared in the early stages of the Thirty Years War, utilized both of these sources. While the principles of the first school had some influence, the practices of war and diplomacy, recognizing the equal sovereignty of territorial states, governed in most cases by absolute monarchs competent to initiate war for 'Reason of State', constituted the basis of international law. The relations of these monarchs were stabilized by the diplomatic system, the network of treaties, the customary rules, and the balance of power. The seas were recognized as outside the domain of states and free to the navigation of all, subject to limitations defined by custom and treaty in time of war. This law, however, was confined to the European states with culture derived from classical antiquity and Christianity. The non-European communities were treated unequally or subjected to colonial regimes.

21

The great changes in international law during the 'classical' period reflected the changes in conditions brought by new inventions (gunpowder and the printing press), new ideologies (science and Protestantism), new contacts (Renaissance and the discoveries), and new political methods (Secularism and Machiavellianism). The world of Newton (1686) was vastly different from that of Dante (1311), and the law of Bynkershoek (1737) was correspondingly different from that of Aquinas (1265). Humanistic principles of justice had given way to mechanistic rules of order.[1]

4. THE NINETEENTH CENTURY

The late eighteenth and nineteenth centuries witnessed changes in international law as momentous as those of the three preceding centuries, also in accommodation to new conditions. Great trading companies, chartered for operations in India, America, and the East and West Indies by Great Britain, the Netherlands, and other European countries, had stimulated overseas trade, colonial rivalry, and naval wars; and had induced treaties and practices defining the freedom of the seas and the rights of neutrals. The recognition of the States General of the Netherlands and the Swiss Confederation by the Treaty of Westphalia (1648), and the revolutions in England (1688), America (1776), and France (1789), weakened the conception of absolute monarchy and changed the conception of the state from a personal to a corporate sovereignty. The state was distinguished from the government and persisted as a jural person through revolutionary changes of government. The ideas of nationalism, as the sentiment unifying the state, and of national interest, as the objective of its policy, naturally followed. Democracy and constitutionalism, manifested by these changes, contributed to the revival of international arbitration (Jay Treaty, 1794) and to movements for peace and disarmament (Rush-Bagot Agreement, 1817), because constitutional democracies, functioning through deliberation and law internally, were less apt than absolute monarchies in the game of power politics.

The admission to the Community of Nations of the United States and the Latin American republics, and, later, of Turkey, Iran, Siam, China, and Japan, extended the concept of the family of nations beyond that of a family of Christian European states, but also led

[1] Wright, *op. cit.*, pp. 196 ff., 332 ff.; Arthur Nussbaum, *A Concise History of the Law of Nations*, New York, Macmillan, 1947, pp. 52 ff.

to ideas of regional differentiation of international law. Ideas of neutrality and neutral obligations tended to be emphasized because of the geographical and political isolation of these regions (especially the Americas) from Europe, which continued to dominate world politics. These ideas were further established by the United States neutrality legislation of 1794 and the conventional neutralizaiton of Switzerland (1815), Belgium (1839), and Luxembourg (1867) as political devices to stabilize the balance of power. The stability of the political equilibrium under the aegis of British sea power and Consultations of the Concert of Europe, the commercial spirit stimulated by British policies of free trade and foreign investment, the opportunities of European states for colonial empire in Asia, Africa, and the Pacific, and the general spirit of liberalism and humanitarianism stemming from the prevalent philosophies of democracy and utilitarianism made the nineteenth century, following the Napoleonic Wars, remarkably peaceful in Europe. After conclusion of the relatively short and relatively mild mid-century wars of nationalism in the Low Countries, the Balkans, Italy, and Germany by 1871, and considering the success of arbitration in the 'Alabama' and other cases in the same year, and the achievement of humanitarian efforts with the Geneva Red Cross Convention of 1864, the future of the Society of Nations seemed bright. Diplomatic efforts to codify the international rules of order at Paris (1856), St. Petersburg (1868), and The Hague (1899 and 1907) registered considerable success. During this period international scholarly bodies to develop international law, such as the Institute of International Law and the International Law Association, were established. Arbitration was frequently utilized to settle international disputes; The Hague Court of Arbitration was established; a few bi-lateral treaties were concluded requiring resort to arbitration in legal disputes; universal standards for the protection of citizens abroad developed through diplomatic and arbitral practice. Public International Unions were organized to regulate postal, telegraph, and railroad communications, to standardize weights and measures, to prevent the spread of infectious diseases, and to protect peoples in colonial areas against slavery and other forms of exploitation. Thus, with relative stability maintained through accepted rules of order, international law advanced in the development of principles of justice and procedures to maintain them.[1]

Outside of Europe the world was much less peaceful. Colonial

[1] Wright, *op. cit.*, pp. 338 ff.; Nussbaum, *op. cit.*, pp. 178 ff.

wars were continuous, and the Civil War in America, the Lopez War in Paraguay, the Taiping Rebellion in China, and the mutiny in India during the 1850's and 1860's were unusually ferocious and destructive; they cost ten times more lives than all the wars in Europe together during the century from Waterloo to the Marne.[1] The rules of order and principles of justice which under conditions of balance of power had contributed unusual stability and prosperity to Europe were not similarly effective throughout the world.[2]

At the beginning of the twentieth century, international rules of order called for respect by states in time of peace for the territorial integrity, political independence, and right to diplomatic immunity of other states, qualified by a limited right to use force in defence or reprisals; for observance of the law of war during a 'state of war' which states were legally free to establish; observance by belligerents of neutral rights at sea and by neutrals of impartiality, abstention by the government and prevention of assistance from their territory to either belligerent. These were the basic rules of international law, in considerable measure codified in the Vienna Protocol (1815); the Declarations of Paris (1856), St. Petersburg (1868), and London (1909); and the Conventions of Geneva (1864, 1906) and The Hague (1899, 1907). They sought to mitigate war and to prevent its spread, but not generally to eliminate it. Limitations on war-making had, however, been suggested at the Hague conferences by codification of procedures of pacific settlement, prohibition of force for debt collecting, and formalities for initiating war. International law consisted mainly of positive rules of order, though arbitral tribunals had utilized general principles of justice in dealing with particular disputes, especially those concerning boundaries, freedom of the seas, the protection of nationals abroad, and reparation for injuries.[3]

International law had ceased to be a law confined to the Christian states of Europe. It had become worldwide, but the Oriental states still suffered from the inequality of extraterritoriality, and the colonial system still extended to more than a quarter of the world's

[1] Estimated from statistics in Lewis F. Richardson, *Statistics of Deadly Quarrels*, Pittsburgh, Boxwood Press; Chicago, Quadrangle Books, 1960, pp. 40 ff.; Wright, 'The Historic Circumstances of Enduring Peace', *Annual Report*, American Historical Association, 1942, Washington, 1944, vol. 3, pp. 363 ff.; *ibid.*, *A Study of War*, pp. 645 ff.

[2] Wright, 'Asian Experience and International Law', *International Studies* (Quarterly Journal of the Indian School of International Studies), July, 1959, vol. 1, pp. 77 ff.

[3] H. Lauterpacht, *Private Law Sources and Analogies of International Law*, 1927; W. Evans Darby, *International Tribunals*, 4th ed., London, 1904, pp. 769 ff.

population. The system of international law on the eve of World War I appeared to Europeans to establish a permanent order of international relations, but conditions had been developing which that law could not control and to which it could only adapt itself by radical changes.

5. WORLD WARS

The changed conditions accompanying and following World War I (1914–1919) brought more changes in international law than had the preceding three centuries. For the first time the Community of Nations sought to organize itself so as to master changing conditions in the interest of values deemed essential to human happiness and progress. Such organization had been proposed by writers such as Emeric Cruce (1623), William Penn (1685), the Abbé St. Pierre (1713), Jeremy Bentham (1789) and Immanuel Kant (1795), and had been experimented with by the great powers in the conference system after the Napoleonic Wars, in the Public International Unions, and in the Hague conferences, but these efforts had not been successful in attacking the problem of war.[1]

World War I indicated that new means of communication and war; weakening sea power and developing air power; new industrial developments augmenting the power of the United States and Japan relative to Europe; and new ideological developments introducing Communism and Fascism, stimulating nationalism, and putting colonialism on the defensive, had all weakened the nineteenth-century balance of power beyond repair. These changes had also increased the destructiveness of war so as to threaten economic and social progress, and had so augmented the concept of military necessity that the laws of war and neutrality could not be relied upon. As a result the conviction became widespread that war itself must be eliminated. The unorganized balance-of-power system must be converted into an organization for collective security. In the treaties ending the war, the powers committed themselves to the Covenant of the League of Nations, intended to prevent war and to foster international co-operation.

The disintegration of the Hapsburg Empire; the refusal of the United States to ratify the Covenant; the differences between Great Britain and France over European reconstruction; the revolutions to

---

[1] Sylvester J. Hemleben, *Plans for World Peace Through Six Centuries*, University of Chicago Press, 1943.

the left in Russia and China and to the right in Italy, Germany, and Spain; the rise of nationalism in Eastern Europe, the Middle East, and Asia; and the economic collapse arising from war costs, reparations, and inflation created such problems of readjustment that neither the League's facilities for peaceful change nor the facilities for mobilizing force behind the *status quo* formulated in the peace treaties could cope with them. The diplomatic activity by the great powers to maintain the power equilibrium by traditional methods proved equally ineffective, and the dissatisfied powers, seeking to revolutionize the international system to their own advantage, combined in the 'Axis' to destroy the League and to initiate World War II.

During the inter-war period, international law faced a crisis. Some jurists and statesmen, looking back at 1914, sought to utilize the League of Nations to preserve, under the old international law, the territorial *status quo* established by the treaties. Others conceived the League of Nations as a means not only for preventing war but also for ameliorating colonialism and economic discrimination, for freeing trade, for protecting minorities, and for transferring territory, when such transfer was supported by world opinion manifested by votes in the League Assembly and by the opinion of the inhabitants of the territory manifested by a plebiscite.[1] The League registered some successes in implementing this progressive conception of international law, but the magnitude of the problems and the ambivalence of its principal members doomed these efforts to eventual failure, and World War II began. The old rules of order controlling war under the balance of power had become obsolete, new rules of order eliminating war under collective security had not become established, and the principles of justice set forth in the Covenant were not sufficiently accepted to be reliable.

World War II manifested, even more decisively than World War I, the obsoleteness of the old international law. The rules of war and neutrality were more flagrantly violated than they had been in the earlier war. New instruments of war, especially the submarine, the tank, the bombing aeroplane, and finally the atomic bomb, facilitating the practice of 'total war', made it clear that war was incompatible with the continuance of civilization. The subsequent development

---

[1] President Wilson proposed such a procedure in his first draft of the Covenant but it was greatly attenuated in Article 19 as it finally appeared. See Wright, 'Article 19 of the League of Nations Covenant', *Proceedings*, American Society of International Law, April, 1936, p. 65; Hunter Miller, 'The Drafting of the Covenant', vol. 2, p. 12.

of supersonic jet planes, missiles, satellites, and nuclear fusion bombs has made it probable that war is incompatible with human survival. National movements in Asia and Africa spelled the doom of colonialism. The barbarities of Nazi persecutions and massacres developed a demand to subordinate national sovereignty to human rights. The awareness of great and increasing differences in standards of living created a conviction in both the developed and the under-developed countries that political stability required a reduction of these economic differences. At the same time the differences between rival ideologies, each convinced that it alone could solve the world's problems, and the effort of each to organize superior power, made it clear that stability even more required a reduction or accommodation of these ideological differences.

6. THE NEW INTERNATIONAL LAW

These new conditions led to more positive efforts to formulate and maintain new rules of international law by effective organization. Such instruments as the Nuremberg Charter (1945), the United Nations Charter (1945), the Constitutions of UNESCO and other Specialized Agencies, the Universal Declaration of Human Rights (1948), the Genocide Convention (1948), the Uniting for Peace Resolution (1950) and the Declaration on the granting of Independence to Colonial Countries and Peoples (1960) gave positive expression and commitment to the new principles of international law which were inherent in the League of Nations Covenant; in League resolutions and conventions on collective security, aggression, pacific settlement, minorities, and mandates; and in the Kellogg-Briand Peace Pact of 1929.[1]

These new principles may be defined as follows:

(a) *The outlawry of war*. The old concept of war as a condition which any sovereign state could initiate at discretion, during which the belligerents were equally entitled to settle their conflict by armed force, was abolished by the Pact and the Charter. Under these instruments, if hostilities occurred, belligerents, if either failed to accept a cease-fire, were not legally equal. One was an aggressor, the other a defender, and third states were not free to be neutral; they should do nothing to assist the aggressor or to hamper the defender. Furthermore, the aggressor could gain no fruits from his aggression, but must compensate for the damage his forces had committed and

[1] Wright, *Contemporary International Law: A Balance Sheet*, Random House, New York, 1955; *Problems of Stability and Progress in International Relations*, Berkeley, California, 1954, pp. 251 ff.

27

must accept the criminal liability of his leaders who had initiated aggression. War was no longer a duel, tolerated by law, but a crime which the law sought to prevent.[1]

(b) *The self-determination of peoples.* Substantial groups with a national character desiring to govern themselves and able to do so should be accorded self-government or independence. Colonialism was to be liquidated and all states, new and old, were to be equal under international law. This principle has guided the political organs of the United Nations dealing with trusteeship and non-self-governing territories. Whether it can be reduced to rules of law sufficiently precise to admit of judicial application is doubtful, though the 'obligation' of states that administer non-self-governing territories 'to develop self-government' is specified in the Charter (Article 73).[2]

(c) *Respect for human rights.* The state is for man, not man for state. Heretofore states have been responsible to other states for the fair treatment of nationals of the latter in their territory. Under certain treaties states have assumed responsibility for the humane treatment of aborigines and others of their nationals liable to abuse, and for assuring respect for civil and cultural rights of racial, religious, and linguistic minorities. Under the law of war states have been responsible for observing certain humane rules in the treatment of enemy soldiers, prisoners of war, and the inhabitants of occupied territories. A general 'pledge' such as that in the Charter (Article 56) to 'take joint and separate action in co-operation with the Organization' to achieve 'universal respect for, and observance of, human rights and fundamental freedoms for all without distinction as to race, sex, language, or religion' is, however, a novelty. Here again there is doubt whether the Charter 'pledge' even as interpreted by the Universal Declaration of Human Rights is sufficiently precise for judicial application, and efforts to define it by concrete 'covenants of human rights' have not yet been successful except in limited areas such as Western Europe.[3]

(d) *The personality of international organizations.* The Community

---

[1] Wright, 'The Prevention of Aggression', *American Journal of International Law*, July, 1956, vol. 50, pp. 514 ff.

[2] *Ibid.*, 'Recognition and Self-Determination', *Proceedings*, American Society of International Law, April, 1954, pp. 23 ff.

[3] *Ibid.*, 'National Courts and Human Rights: The Fujii Case', *American Journal of International Law*, January, 1951, vol. 45, pp. 62 ff.; 'Freedom and Human Rights under International Law', in *Aspects of Liberty*, M. R. Konvitz and C. Rossiter, eds., Cornell University Press, 1958, pp. 181 ff.; H. Lauterpacht, *International Law and Human Rights*, London, Stevens, 1950.

of Nations constitutes a legal personality organized in the United Nations, and the Specialized Agencies, with rights and duties, powers and responsibilities, to assure respect, by its members, and even by non-members, for its principles. All of the legal deductions to be drawn from this conception are not clear, though the International Court of Justice has found that the United Nations is entitled to demand reparation from a state—even a non-member—responsible for injury to a United Nations agent.[1] Many other qualifications of the sovereignty of states will doubtless be found to flow from this principle, as for instance the right of the United Nations to conduct investigations in the territory of states in case violations by members of their international obligations are alleged and to negotiate through the Secretary General to settle such disputes.[2] These principles of the new international law considerably modify the traditional scope of the territorial sovereignty, and the right of self-help, of sovereign states. The institutions of the Community of Nations have not, however, been able to give them full effect. Conditions of national self-assertion, ideological difference, power rivalry, and mutual suspicion have not been subdued by the United Nations.

Of these four principles, the first and last are designed to be rules of order but have not been sufficiently defined or organized to assure the functioning of collective security. They have indeed been in a measure superseded by the development of power blocs, permitted by the Charter provisions concerning collective self-defence but resulting in such a bi-polarization of power in the world that the operation of collective security has been seriously hampered. Peace actually depends upon an unstable balance of terror, rather than on collective security, though the latter has functioned to stop most border hostilities.

Respect for human rights is a principle of justice which, however, has not been reconciled with the sovereign equality of states, said to constitute the basis of the United Nations as it was of traditional international law. Self-determination of peoples has functioned as a political rather than a legal principle. Closely related to these principles of justice is the duty of states to co-operate for social, cultural, and economic welfare. The activities of the Specialized Agencies and

---

[1] 'Reparation for Injuries Suffered in the Service of the United Nations (Count Bernadotte Case)', *I.C.J. Report*, 1949, pp. 174, 183.
[2] Commission to Study the Organization of Peace, *Strengthening the United Nations* (A. N. Holcombe, ed.), New York, Harper, 1957, pp. 36, 78 ff.

the programmes of economic assistance seek to implement this duty by concrete agreements and actions. Such a duty, however, dependent as it is on voluntary action, must be regarded as moral rather than legal in character.

In my next lecture attention will be given to the conditions of the world to which these principles must adapt themselves if they are to survive.

Chapter III

INTERNATIONAL LAW AND CONTEMPORARY CONDITIONS

1. LAW AND SOCIETY

LAW is a body of rules, principles, standards, and public policies establishing relations within a society. It attempts to reconcile the values inherent in the culture with the interests of the persons whom it seeks to control; the aspirations of the people with the inertias of custom; the logical consistency demanded by reason with the wisdom derived from experience; and the policies of the society with its capabilities in relation to the circumstances which it faces. Law thus tries to synthesize the whole and the parts, the desired and the actual, the rational and the real, the ends and the means.

Human values, aspirations, reasons, and purposes, whether social or individual, progressive or conservative, abstract or concrete, active or passive, are always confronted by conditions—physical, biological, psychological, and social—which tend to frustrate their achievement. Law seeks to mobilize the force of society behind the policies, principles, and rules which it recognizes in order to overcome these frustrating conditions. To this end an advanced system of law formulates the values and interests it will protect, appraises the encroachments on them with consideration of motives and intentions, affixes consequences to encroachments thus appraised, and specifies procedures for applying these formulations, appraisals, and consequences to actual situations.

The purpose of law is, therefore, to maintain certain values, goals, and interests so that they will be realized in the actual behaviour of its members and its agents. Hopes for the future and conditions growing from the past each play a part in both the application and the development of the law. *Lex lata* and *lex ferenda* cannot be wholly separated.

Law and society reciprocally influence each other. *Ubi societas, ibi jus.* In primitive societies law must adapt itself to social and technological changes, which, apart from natural catastrophe or military conquest, usually take place slowly. But as man progresses

31

in his capacity to control nature, both physical and human, law exerts a positive influence, adapting society to the values which it sanctions. This is necessary because progress implies increasingly rapid social change, guidance of which by law is the price of stability and predictability. Thus, as society becomes progressive, the law is less bound to material and social conditions and is more a reflection of human values and purposes.

2. INTERNATIONAL LAW AND DIPLOMACY

The society of nations has been a primitive society. The self-determined interests of its members have dominated over formally accepted principles of justice; the customs of the past have dominated over aspirations for the future; the experience of history has dominated over the dictates of reason; and the conditions of international politics have dominated over purposes expressed in general conventions. But this dominance of conditions over values has been challenged. The development of facilities for central communication, of treaties formulating accepted principles, of co-operation toward common goals, of organizations to maintain international order and justice, have begun to give mankind as a whole the capability of controlling the conditions of international life by law.

However, many contemporary writers on international relations have minimized the importance of international law. They have declared that governments ought, or, in any case, will, be guided by what they deem the 'national interest', even though it requires a departure from international law, or morality. This attitude, associated with Machiavelli's famous advice to princes, has sometimes been called 'realism' in distinction from 'idealism'.[1]

Others, however, have insisted that international law can be a guide to determining both the means and the ends of a wise foreign policy, and that it cannot be opposed to the national interest because its general observance is a national interest. Grotius asserts:

For just as the national who violates the law of his country in order to obtain an immediate advantage, breaks down that by which the advan-

---

[1] John H. Herz, *Political Realism and Political Idealism*, University of Chicago Press, 1951, p. 18; Leo Perla discusses the views of George Kennan, Hans Morgenthau, Dean Acheson, John Foster Dulles, and others on this subject (*Can We End the Cold War?*, New York, Macmillan, 1960, pp. 26 ff.); and Percy Corbett examines the prevalence of 'realism' in practice (*Law in Diplomacy*, Princeton University Press, 1959, p. 272).

tages of himself and his posterity are for all future time assured, so the state which transgresses the laws of nature and of nations cuts away also the bulwarks which safeguard its own future peace.[1]

According to this theory, international law indicates the means that states may employ for achieving foreign policy goals without inviting such criticism or even hostility from other states as to frustrate that achievement. It is also said that international law can be of great assistance in determining foreign policy goals or national interests, especially in a highly interdependent world in which all states are vulnerable to attack. A world of unstable equilibrium and a race in arms of increasing destructiveness, generating high tensions, is undoubtedly a dangerous place to live in. No state, even the most powerful, can, it is said, be secure unless the world as a whole is organized to assure the peaceful coexistence of all.[2] International law describes the conditions of such a world.

The actual use of international law by foreign offices has, however, varied among different states at different periods in the history of each. The Moore and Hackworth *Digests of International Law* disclose numerous instances in which the United States and other countries have relied on international law in the conduct of foreign relations. Lord McNair's compilation of opinions of the Law Officers of the Crown during several centuries indicates that the British Foreign Office usually sought legal advice before reaching a decision.[3] These compilations, however, do not always disclose the actual influence of such advice on the decisions eventually taken. Professor Percy Corbett in his historical survey of the practices of Great Britain, the United States, and the Soviet Union concludes that, in each,

---

[1] Grotius, *De Jure Belli ac Pacis* (Carnegie Edition), Prolegomena, sec. 18.

[2] I have discussed in *A Study of War* (University of Chicago Press, 1942) the need for, and the difficulty of developing, a world point of view in relation to the conception (pp. 972 ff.), the myth (pp. 1035 ff.), the organization (pp. 1058 ff.), and the human advantages (pp. 1350 ff.) of a universal society; in relation to the balance of power (pp. 818 ff.), the state of opinion (pp. 1081 ff.), and the expectations of violence (pp. 1227 ff.) in the contemporary world; and in *The Study of International Relations* (New York, 1955) I have examined the position on this subject of the disciplines, among others, of international relations (pp. 23 ff.), communications (pp. 274 ff.), education (pp. 316 ff.), sociology (pp. 398 ff.), psychology (pp. 423 ff.), and ethics (pp. 445 ff.); as well as the historical conceptions (pp. 484 ff.), and practical values (pp. 65 ff., 570 ff.) of such a point of view. See also *The Strengthening of International Law* (pp. 27 ff.) on the 'International Mind'.

[3] J. B. Moore, *A Digest of International Law*, 8 vols., Washington, 1906; Green Hackworth, *A Digest of International Law*, 8 vols., Washington, 1940; A. D. McNair, *The Law of Treaties*, New York, 1938; *ibid.*, *International Law Opinions*, 3 vols., London, 1956.

international law was employed less as a guide to foreign policy than as propaganda seeking to justify policy decisions reached for other reasons.

The enthusiasm reserved by Soviet jurists for the Socialist importations into the body of international rule, and their constant denunciation of any legal propositions tending to limit Soviet sovereignty, reveal the essential rejection of world community under a legal system not wholly of their own making. But in the democracies also the notion of national interest still outweighs the claims of a world community subject to law. In matters that concern them deeply, though the law is still invoked, the specific rule always supports the national case, and no authority is permitted to gainsay the national interpretation. In these circumstances, with political considerations dictating the content of the rule, it becomes clear that law is being made a tool of policy, and the notion of an objectively binding system abandoned in practice.[1]

Professor Charles De Visscher insists on the importance of international law, and recognizes the danger to civilization if a wide gap develops between 'precept and practice' and between 'formal concepts and realities' in international relations, and urges that the content of international law be continually influenced by a realistic appraisal of the national interests of states as they interpret them.

The hour is not one for doctrinal generalizations, moving in the rhythm of a transcendental logic, or for brilliant systematizations in which intellectual ingenuity often counts for more than respect for facts. It is rather one that challenges us to recognize the limits which in our day dependence of international law on the historical forms of power and distribution sets to its effectiveness, and to seek in the human ends of power the moderating principle that may develop aspirations to international collaboration. Every renewed recognition of the foundations of power stimulates a renewal of values; every return to the realities holds promise of effectiveness.[2]

George Kennan, former chairman of the Policy Planning Committee of the U.S. State Department, has expressed the opinion that there has been too much 'moralism and legalism' in United States foreign policy.[3] Thus in the popular dichotomy between 'realists' and 'idealists' he appears to align himself with the former. These terms are highly ambiguous. Realism has meant different

---

[1] Corbett, *op. cit.*, p. 107.

[2] Charles De Visscher, *Theory and Reality in Public International Law*, Princeton University Press, 1957, p. 364.

[3] George Kennan, *American Diplomacy, 1900–1950*, University of Chicago Press, 1951, p. 95.

things as applied to Plato and Machiavelli, and idealism has meant different things as applied to Bishop Berkeley and President Wilson. Realism has meant both insistence upon the importance of ideas compared with appearances, and insistence upon the importance of power compared with ideals. Idealism has meant both dependence of the objective world upon subjective interpretations, and the superior influence, in the long run, of generally accepted values over temporary and local capabilities. It would appear both realistic and idealistic to choose a decision only after considering the relevant values and the favourable or detrimental effect of each possible alternative upon them. Consequently, appropriate policy might be called 'realistic idealism' or, if one prefers, 'idealistic realism'. So long as man is both an actor and an observer, endowed with reason, he must concern himself with, not only what is, but also what ought to be, and what can be, seeking to bridge the ever-present gaps between them by the application of intelligence.[1] This problem, however, presents exceptional difficulties in the international field, composed as it is of many different cultures, ideologies, and religions, each passionately devoted to its own convictions of what ought to be. With so many pictures of the perfect world, how is it possible for strife to be avoided and justice to be administered?[2]

In criticizing American legalism and moralism, George Kennan may have meant that American Secretaries of State and the American public have been too much inclined to deduce foreign policy decisions from general principles without consideration of the probable consequences of their application under existing conditions. He may, therefore, have been urging more inductive, strategic, and political thinking and less deductive, ideological, and theoretical thinking in deciding what to do. If this was his meaning, many would agree with him. Valuable as general principles may be, if they are to serve as guides to action, they must be formulated pragmatically with reference to consequences and applied in the light of the facts of the particular situation.[3]

Kennan may, however, have been deploring the tendency which

[1] See Quincy Wright, *World Politics*, October, 1952, vol. 5, pp. 116 ff.; *Yale Review*, Autumn, 1951, vol. 41, pp. 137 ff.; *American Historical Review*, October, 1957, reviewing the books by Herz, Corbett, and De Visscher mentioned above.

[2] Justice Oliver Wendell Holmes in *Holmes-Pollock Letters* (Mark D. Howe, ed., Harvard University Press, 1941), vol. 2, p. 36; Percy Corbett, *Postwar Worlds*, New York, Farrar & Rinehart, 1942, pp. 7 ff.

[3] Wright, *Problems of Stability and Progress in International Relations*, University of California Press, 1954, pp. 167 ff.

Americans, and indeed the citizens of most countries, have often exhibited, of regarding their particular moral or legal standards as the only moral or legal standards possible, unaware that others, with equal sincerity but different conditions and traditions, adhere to other standards. Here again many would agree with him. In the field of foreign policy sophisticated observers would usually recognize that standards are not absolute but relative to the situation. They would try to avoid the provincialism which interprets our tribe, our city, or our nation as the world, and our period of history as eternity.[1]

It is possible that Kennan intended to criticize a combination of complacency and intolerance, frequently said to characterize American opinion. Though aware of other legal and moral systems, Americans are often said to assume that their system is superior and that their government should compel others to accept the benefits of that system for their own good. Such an arrogance, which lurks in the phrase occasionally used, 'the American Century', has also characterized other peoples and has led to ideological wars such as that of Islam, continued intermittently for 1000 years with Christendom in the West and with Zoroastrianism and Hinduism in the East, and that of Catholicism with Protestantism for more than a hundred, ending in the Thirty Years War of the seventeenth century. If legalism and moralism mean crusading with such results, few would commend such attitudes, especially in the age of atomic weapons. Superior ideas, religious or secular, should, especially in our age, be tested and spread by discussion and persuasion, not by the sword. That imperialism—religious and ideological as well as economic and political—is outmoded seems to be recognized in theory even by the Communists.[2]

George Kennan may have been assuming that Americans frequently profess ideals of law and morality which they do not practise, thus exhibiting the gap between profession and practice deplored by De Visscher.[3] If legalism and moralism mean hypocrisy, they certainly are not admirable traits, though they may give evidence of a lag of static values behind changing technologies and opportunties. If Kennan was criticizing the invocation or observance of ancient rules and principles no longer adapted to the present conditions, as very

[1] Wright, *The Study of International Relations*, New York, Appleton-Century-Crofts, 1955, pp. 442, 451 ff.

[2] *Ibid.*, 'International Law and Ideology', *American Journal of International Law*, October, 1954, vol. 48, pp. 616 ff.

[3] Above p. 34, n. 2; Wright, *A Study of War*, pp. 164, 355, 357, 386.

possibly he was, there may also be merit in his indictment. Archaism is not useful in conducting foreign policy.[1]

To summarize, if Kennan was criticizing Americans for a lack of realism in failing to consider the consequences of alternative courses of action, for a lack of sophistication in ignoring the existence of competing value systems, for a lack of humility in asserting their superiority, for a lack of sincerity in relating professions to actions, or for a lack of common sense in citing or adhering to obsolete principles or precedents, many would agree with him. If, however, he was saying that foreign policy must be Machiavellian, that morality and law have no role in this field, he was on debatable ground. He probably intended 'moralism' and 'legalism' to mean something different from morality and law, just as 'historicism' means something different from history, 'socialism' something different from society, and 'nationalism' something different from nationality. Leaving aside the problem of international morality, Kennan's criticism emphasizes, at least, that to be useful international law must be closely related to the conditions of the international community in which it is to be applied, whether as a rule of order or a principle of justice.

3. CONDITIONS OF THE WORLD

In considering international law, it is therefore pertinent to examine the actual conditions of the world of states today. What are those conditions?

(a) There is one world materially, in the sense that every considerable people is continually aware of what is going on everywhere; most are dependent on others for markets or raw materials; all are vulnerable to aggression from border states or nuclear attack; and many are vulnerable to subversive intervention intended to displace their government or way of life, through paramilitary activity such as espionage, sabotage, and assassination, through secret infiltration and corruption, or through public propaganda.[2]

---

[1] Such a lag has been regarded as a major cause of the decline and fall of civilizations (A. J. Toynbee, *A Study of History*, Oxford, 1939, vol. 4, p. 133), of social maladjustment (W. F. Ogburn, *Social Change*, New York, Viking, 1937, pp. 208 ff.), and of war (Wright, *A Study of War*, p. 1284).

[2] 'Our present defence policy admits of three military threats to the free world. Two of them we call by the same names as our opponents do, nuclear war and limited war. The third, which we call indirect aggression, is known to its practitioners as wars of liberation.' Harlan Cleveland, Assistant Secretary of State for International Organizational Affairs, address, Syracuse, New York, May 7,

(*b*) There are many worlds, morally, in the sense of the commitment of each people to a nationality, to a religion, to an ideology, or to a way of life which it regards as superior to and incapable of reconciliation with others, and which it hopes may eventually be more widely adopted. While most states have formally agreed to the United Nations Charter and other instruments formulating certain basic principles of justice, including non-intervention and respect for one another's sovereignty, and while philosophers have detected a possibility of synthesizing competing ideologies in universal principles, popular opinion, on both sides of the 'iron curtain', has remained sceptical in regard to either geographical segregation or philosophical synthesis of these varied opinions and values.[1]

(*c*) This condition has generated a system of power blocs engaged in an arms race which has resulted in mutual fear, increasing tension, and widespread expectations of general war, if not through deliberate attack, then through pre-emptive attack, accident, miscalculation, the escalation of small wars, or the spread of nuclear weapons to irresponsible powers.[2]

(*d*) Governments have sought solutions by maintaining nuclear weapons and bases to deter deliberate attack, by maintaining second-strike capability to stabilize the balance of terror, and by maintaining mobile conventional weapons and support for local defence forces to deter or stop border hostilities. They have also sought agreements for arms control with adequate inspection against surprise attack, against the spread of nuclear weapons and the danger of fallout from nuclear testing, and against continuance of the arms race by reduction of categories of weapons.[3]

1961. According to Henry Gemmill, some planners in Washington would 'match and if possible surpass the Communists in subversion, infiltration, and other undeclared warfare' as a supplement to 'massive retaliation' and 'flexible response'. *Wall Street Journal*, May 16, 1961.

[1] Above p. 33, n. 2; F. S. C. Northrop, *Philosophical Anthropology and Practical Politics*, New York, Macmillan, 1960, pp. 13, 354.

[2] Henry A. Kissinger, *Nuclear Weapons and Foreign Policy*, New York, Council on Foreign Relations, 1959; Samuel P. Huntington, *Arms Races: Prerequisites and Results*, Harvard University Graduate School of Public Administration, 1958; Albert J. Wohlstetter, 'The Delicate Balance of Terror', *Foreign Affairs*, January, 1959, vol. 37, pp. 211 ff.; Fred C. Icle, *Bulletin of the Atomic Scientists*, December, 1960, p. 394; Sir Charles Snow, address to the American Association for the Advancement of Science, New York, December 27, 1960; Bertrand Russell, *Common Sense and Nuclear Warfare*, New York, 1959.

[3] *Ibid.*, and Bernard Brodie, *Strategy in the Missile Age*, Princeton University Press, 1959; Gen. Maxwell Taylor, *The Uncertain Trumpet*, New York, 1959; Morton Halperin, *Nuclear Weapons and Limited War*, Harvard University Center for International Affairs, July, 1960; Seymour Melman, ed., *Inspection*

(*e*) No arms control agreements have been reached, in spite of continuous negotiation since World War II. Hostilities and revolutions have occurred in many states. Tensions have been increasing, and the Communist bloc of states has been gaining over the Western democracies in relative power position, whether measured by conventional arms, missiles, nuclear weapons, or military technology; by technical education, industrial potential, available resources, or population; by apparent solidarity of the members of the bloc and confidence in the future; and even by reputation for peacefulness and progressiveness among the uncommitted states of the world. Whatever may be the causes of the gain of Communism in relative power position, the fact can hardly be denied.[1]

(*f*) The United Nations has succeeded in ending hostilities in Greece, Iran, Indonesia, Kashmir, Palestine, Korea, and the Suez by calling for a cease-fire, and special conferences have similarly dealt with hostilities in Vietnam and Laos. The United Nations has succeeded in moderating internal hostilities in the Congo. However, neither the United Nations nor other conferences have been able to solve the disputes which caused these hostilities in most cases, with the result that unstable armistice lines continue to divide Germany, Korea, Vietnam, Kashmir, and Palestine, and sporadic hostilities have occurred in the off-shore islands of Quemoy and Matsu, in the Straits of Formosa, and in the Congo. These inconsistencies in the will of states to avoid war and their will to settle disputes are manifested by their attribution to the United Nations of formal powers of decision to maintain international peace and security, but only recommendatory capacity for the settlement of international disputes.[2]

(*g*) The principal governments have publicly professed a desire for reduction of tensions, for general disarmament, and for peaceful coexistence of all states, implying mutual respect for territorial integrity and political independence; but they have continued to

for Disarmament, New York, Columbia University Press, 1958; Philip Noel-Baker, *The Arms Race: A Programme for World Disarmament*, London, Stevens, 1958; Grenville Clark and Louis B. Sohn, *World Peace Through World Law*, Harvard University Press, 1958; Gerald Holton, ed., 'Arms Control', *Daedalus*, American Academy of Arts and Sciences, Fall, 1960.

[1] Gen. Taylor, *op. cit.*, pp. 131 ff.; Victor H. Wallace, ed., *Paths to Peace*, Melbourne University Press, 1957, p. 210.

[2] See United Nations Charter, chaps. VI and VII; Commission to Study the Organization of Peace, 11th Report, *Organizing Peace in the Nuclear Age*, A. N. Holcombe, ed., New York University Press, 1959, pp. 37 ff.

engage in illegal espionage, subversive intervention, military assistance, and acts of aggression.[1]

(h) Such peace as there is rests on an unstable balance of terror, with the hope of either peoples or governments for a more stable peace of mutual trust decreasing as one effort after another of the great power blocs to reach agreement has failed. Even in the United States there appears to be increasing support for resort to paramilitary operations and subversive intervention, imitating methods in which Communist governments have long displayed facility.[2]

These conditions are unfavourable both to law and to democracy. The two are related. Democracy, the essence of which is deliberation in decision-making and respect for individual rights, is at a disadvantage in a jungle world called by Thomas Hobbes a 'state of nature' in which everyone is at war with everyone else and the life of man is nasty, brutish, and short.[3] Democracy has never flourished unless protected by geographical barriers, by a stable balance of power, or by a reign of law. Because these conditions have not been frequent, the emergence of democracies has been rare in history. Not only can highly centralized governments, controlling the economy, act with secrecy, dispatch, and ruthlessness, but such governments today have interior lines enabling them to initiate border hostilities in widely separated areas. Because of these advantages, manifested by their rapid gains in power position since World War II, the Communist powers may not favour the strengthening of law which would tend to equalize the conditions of competition between democracies and dictatorships.[4]

In spite of this, the Soviet government continually propagandizes for peace both at home and abroad. It is clearly aware of the devastating effect of nuclear hostilities. It has asserted that Communism is not for export but for imitation. There can be little doubt but that the Soviet people, after their sufferings in World War II, oppose further war and that the Soviet government does not wish to risk

[1] See Commission to Study the Organization of Peace, 12th Report, *Peaceful Coexistence*, New York, June, 1960; Wright, 'Subversive Intervention,' *American Journal of International Law*, July, 1960, vol. 54, p. 521; *ibid.*, 'Intervention and Cuba', *Proceedings*, American Society of International Law, April, 1961; *ibid.*, 'Espionage and the Doctrine of Non-Intervention in Internal Affairs', Ohio State University, 1961.

[2] See p. 37, n. 2.   [3] Thomas Hobbes, *Leviathan* (1951), chap. 13.

[4] Wright, *A Study of War*, pp. 825, 842; *Control of American Foreign Relations*, New York, Macmillan, 1922, pp. 363 ff., 370; Elihu Root, 'The Effect of Democracy on International Law', *Proceedings*, American Society of International Law, 1917, pp. 7 ff.

the destruction of its economic development. Furthermore, it has made clear that it wishes to cut down the expense of heavy armaments in order to develop its civilian economy more rapidly. These attitudes are less evident in the Communist government of China, whose revolution is more recent and whose acquaintance with atomic weapons is not direct. However, the government of Mao Tse-tung has also asserted that force cannot be used for the external expansion of Communism, but only in internal revolutions.

If each side believes that it can present a more attractive model to the peoples of the uncommitted world under conditions of peaceful coexistence of states, the realization of such conditions should not be impossible.

4. CONDITIONS OF PEACE

However, the conditions for such a world of peaceful coexistence differ considerably from the conditions of the actual world. The conditions of peace would seem to include at least the following.

(a) General acceptance by governments and people of peaceful coexistence, and abandonment by each nation and ideology of efforts to create a world beyond its frontiers in its own image. This implies a limitation of crusading activities to fair methods of persuasion, necessarily slow. It is to be observed, however, that most crusading ideologies of the past, whether Christianity, Islam, or democracy, have eventually been content to develop in a limited area and to confine expansion to peaceful methods.

(b) Establishment of a clear picture of a world of peaceful coexistence in the minds of people. The study of international law as it has developed that picture for centuries, and as it has adapted it to current conditions by the rules and principles of the United Nations Charter, might be the best means to this end, though study of more concrete materials of world geography, history, and culture would also contribute. The picture drawn by international law has the advantage that it has been formally accepted by nearly all the states of the world.

(c) The reduction of international tensions through pursuit of policies by each bloc to moderate the arms race and to restore confidence. Defence without provocation, conciliation without appeasement, observance of international law, abstention from intervention, and participation in United Nations measures to stop such interventions by others, would seem suitable guides to such policies.

(*d*) Stabilization of the power equilibrium by the simultaneous decentralization of the great power blocs, rendering them less capable of aggression without weakening them for defence. The pressure of Great Britain upon the United States to refrain from intervention in Southeast Asia in the crisis of 1954, and the pressure of the United States in the United Nations to restrain Great Britain and France from continuing their intervention at Suez in 1956, were hopeful indications of such a trend, as is the apparent pressure by the Soviet Union upon China to exercise restraint in respect to South Korea, Formosa, and Southeast Asia. The extent of such pressure is, however, controversial.

(*e*) The strengthening of collective security by development of United Nations procedures and of a United Nations policing force composed of contingents from small nations to deal with small wars. Such developments have been particularly notable in the Suez and Congo incidents.

(*f*) Co-operation among states to reduce the great disparities in standards of living as between the highly industrialized and the underdeveloped countries by economic assistance programmes, utilizing in so far as possible United Nations agencies in order to avoid competition between the great blocs and the importation of the cold war into the underdeveloped countries.

(*g*) Clarification of basic rules of international order to protect states against violence under present conditions. Definitions and rules capable of application in emergencies to determine the states to be protected (recognition), the violence to be forbidden (aggression), the control of arms necessary to this end (disarmament), and the limitations upon even legitimate uses of force (rules of war) have long occupied the attention of the United Nations, but success has not yet been achieved.

(*h*) Development of procedures of pacific settlement, extension of the jurisdiction of the International Court of Justice, and formulation of basic principles of justice and rules of law to guide the Court and other agencies in settling disputes. Rules to determine the state's domain, nationals, jurisdiction, and agencies; its responsibility for interventions, denials of justice, and negligences injuring others; and the validity, interpretation, and termination of its agreements has been the traditional content of international law. New principles, qualifying the concept of territorial sovereignty by urging respect for human rights, by promoting the self-determination of peoples, and by facilitating co-operation for human welfare, are asserted in the

United Nations Charter and other generally accepted instruments, but these and other principles of justice require elaboration by concrete agreements, juristic activity, or judicial opinion.

5. THE ROLE OF LAW IN THE TRANSITION FROM COLD WAR TO PEACE

Conditions as they actually are and conditions which would maintain a world safe for democracy are very different. To move the world from the first to the second type of conditions implies action on many fronts—educational, diplomatic, military, economic, and legal. Enlightened activity by statesmen, educators, soldiers, businessmen, lawyers, and others is necessary; but law itself, by formulating rules of order and principles of justice, can be a powerful aid to statesmen and others who wish a peaceful world, in which fair competition in ways of life, forms of government, and systems of thought and economy can make for human progress.

The content of international law to establish a world of peaceful coexistence will be considered in the next lecture, but it must be emphasized that international law must be based on consideration of conditions as they are, as well as conditions more conformable to human aspirations. As noted in the early part of this lecture, law, while based on the general acceptance of values, must apply them to conditions which are not wholly favourable to those values. Thus while the unstable balance of power remains, the law must seek to stabilize it, by controlling arms in order to make deterrence effective. It is not to be expected that general disarmament, implying a considerable measure of trust among nations, can emerge immediately. The law must, therefore, seek to organize collective security to prevent aggression, with full realization that such operations cannot deal with cold war issues so long as nuclear power is bi-polarized. So long as distrust prevents wide acceptance of impartial adjudication as the ultimate solution of controversies, the law must seek to limit self-help and to encourage negotiation by providing for mediation, inquiry, conciliation, and conference to assist it, and by formulating generally accepted principles of justice narrowing the gap between disputing states.

Despite the unfavourable conditions of the world for realization of the principles of international law and the United Nations Charter, human ingenuity and reason have at times surmounted great difficulties. It is to be hoped that peoples will not increase the danger of nuclear annihilation by regarding it as unavoidable but will rather bend their efforts and demand that their governments exert themselves to create conditions in which the nations can peacefully coexist under rules of international order, and settle their disputes in accord with principles of justice.

Chapter IV

THE CONTENT OF INTERNATIONAL LAW —RULES OF ORDER

1. LAW, FACTS, AND JUSTICE

IN judicial proceedings law is usually distinguished from facts. In common law proceedings law is for the learned judge, facts for the common-sense jury. The law is thus conceived as an artificial system which the common man cannot deduce from general experience, while facts, which include both observable events and subjective intentions, can be appraised from the common man's experience. However, the two are never wholly distinct. What rules of law are applicable to the facts of a particular case is argued by lawyers on opposing sides. It may even be argued that the facts are so extraordinary that no precise rule of law is applicable and consequently the judge must deduce a rule from broad principles of justice, or must introduce qualifications in an established rule to prevent obvious injustice. On the other hand, facts are frequently uncertain. The evidence is conflicting, witnesses are unreliable; consequently the law has created presumptions or has excluded types of evidence in order to prevent the common sense of the jury from going astray. Thus the law is interpreted, or even made, by the judge's scrutiny of the facts; and the facts are controlled, or sometimes made, by the law, as when jurisdiction was determined by non-rebuttable fictions.

Among jurists, law is distinguished from justice. Law is found in precise and authoritative sources, such as codes, statutes, and judicial precedents. Justice is found in principles and standards said to be inherent in the culture and values of the society, incorporating precepts of the prevailing ideology or religion, and disclosed by the introspection, faith, or reason of ordinary human beings. These sources are said by some positivists to produce results so varied that objective justice, distinct from law, is an illusion or an ideal, which can assume objective form only by a process of juristic or legislative synthesis co-ordinating various subjective concepts of justice and interests into rules of law. Courts, therefore, according to such positivists, should concern themselves only with law (*lex lata*), leaving justice (*lex ferenda*) to the legislature. However, this absolute distinction between law and justice is difficult to maintain in practice, especially in relatively undeveloped legal systems such as international law. The International Law Commission of the United Nations has, in fact, found itself unable or unwilling to specify in which of these categories a proposed rule should be classified. The intent of the Charter (Article 13, paragraph A) and of the Statute of the Commission to distinguish the 'codification' of existing law from its 'progressive development' has proved of limited applicability in practice.

In even well-developed systems, the sources of positive law never provide precise rules for all cases. They leave the judge considerable discretion to apply broad principles stated in constitutions, codes, statutes, judicial precedents, or legal maxims, and to give effect to legislative purposes or public policies. The effort of primitive communities to make basic rules of order precise and objective by codes of 'strict law' are seen, with the progress of culture and the increasing complexity of society, to yield so much injustice that they are interpreted, expanded, and developed by ideas of natural law developed from rational philosophy, of universal law flowing from comparison of diverse legal systems, and of equity appealing to a common sense of justice.

Law, therefore, operates between facts and justice. While striving to realize the values of the culture, it cannot ignore the conditions of the society. In proportion as society is primitive and the problem of order is pressing, law must cleave close to facts and often appear arbitrary and illogical. As society becomes ordered and progressive, law can in a measure control facts in accord with justice and become rational and consistent. Society becomes a work of art, not of nature. In all societies, however, there are some rules aimed at order and others at justice.

Modern international law originated in the practice of warlike princes, claiming territorial sovereignty, to permit their coexistence in a society without central authority.[1] Renaissance jurists applied 'natural law', deduced from Greek and medieval philosophy and Roman law, by analogy to international relations, establishing principles of international justice.[2] The effort of later jurists to

---

[1] Julius Gebel, Jr., *The Equality of States, A Study in the History of Law*, New York, Columbia University Press, 1923, pp. 47, 58.

[2] Edwin D. Dickinson, *The Equality of States in International Law*, Harvard University Press, 1920, pp. 3 ff.

distinguish these evidences of justice from positive international law, established by convention or custom, was never wholly successful. Grotius recognized both custom (*jus gentium*) and reason (*jus naturale*) as sources of international law, and, in spite of the dominant positivism of the nineteenth century, the Statute of the International Court of Justice establishes 'general principles of law recognized by civilized nations' and 'the teachings of the most highly qualified publicists of various nations' as sources of international law to be utilized if applicable conventions, customs, or precedents do not provide a clear rule, or provide a rule the unqualified application of which would seem clearly unjust in the circumstances. It has been pointed out that arbitral tribunals have often utilized principles found in such sources;[1] and in the original drafting of the Statute of the Permanent Court of International Justice it was agreed that such sources must be included, in order that the Court might not be obliged to declare itself *non liquet* because of the absence of an applicable rule established by convention or custom. Furthermore, while conventions 'establishing rules expressly recognized by the contesting states' are placed in the statute as the first source of international law, the rules to be found in treaties often lack precision and have the character of general principles or standards. This is notably true in the United Nations Charter, which, apart from rules stating the organization and procedure of its principal organs and certain rules prohibiting the use of force, declares purposes and principles of considerable generality but intended to modify many of the rules of international law established by custom and treaty in the past (Article 103).

To understand the scope and content of contemporary international law it must be appreciated that, while it is law designed to control conduct, not merely to explain it, because of the imperfection of its sanctions it has had to accommodate itself rather closely to the facts of international relations. *Ex factis jus oritur.*[2] Furthermore, while it seeks to maintain principles of justice, for the same reason, its prime concern has been to maintain rules of order to facilitate the coexistence of states in a world in which all have been insecure. As indicated in my first lecture, its primary function has been, and

---

[1] Hersh Lauterpacht, *Private Law Sources and Analogies of International Law*, London, Longmans, 1927.

[2] Lauterpacht has pointed out that the principle of justice 'jus ex injuria non oritur', suggesting non-recognition of illegal conquests, must be balanced by this rule of order suggesting recognition of an established fact. *Recognition in International Law*, Cambridge University Press, 1947, p. 427.

continues under the Charter to be, to assure 'the territorial integrity and political independence of states'.[1] Each is to be secure in the enjoyment of 'sovereign equality'.[2] The primary duty of each is to settle its international disputes peacefully[3] and 'to refrain from the threat or use of force in their international relations'[4] and to co-operate with the United Nations to prevent violation of this duty.[5]

The second function, indicated by the history of international law, implied by the text of the Charter, and specified by the Statute of the Court, is to facilitate the just settlement of international disputes. To codify and develop principles, in the light of past acceptances and present needs of the Society of Nations, has been the task of the International Law Commission; and, in fact, as pointed out by the late Judge Lauterpacht, the clarification and development of international law has been a most important function of the International Court of Justice, perhaps more important than the settlement of disputes.[6] But what is the relation between justice to the state and justice to the individual? How can the equal sovereignty of each state to determine the rights of its citizens be reconciled with the protection of human rights from abuse by the state? While the requirements of

---

[1] Charter, Article 2, paragraph 4.

[2] *Ibid.*, Article 2, paragraph 1.

[3] *Ibid.*, Article 2, paragraph 3. Respect is paid to 'justice' in this paragraph upon the insistence of the smaller states at the San Francisco Conference.

[4] *Ibid.*, Article 2, paragraph 4. The further explanation 'against the territorial integrity or political independence of any state, or in any other manner inconsistent with the purposes of the United Nations' seems intended to emphasize the prohibition of any territorial invasion or attack on the public forces of another state not explicitly authorized by the Charter. Julius Stone, however, finds in this phrase a permission for military reprisals, apparently on the contention, made unsuccessfully by Mussolini in the Corfu incident of 1923, that an invasion for that purpose, and not for conquest, is not a violation of territorial integrity or political independence (*Aggression and World Order*, New York, 1958). To the contrary, Sir John Fischer Williams held that 'forcible entry' is a wrongful aggression 'in breach of the guarantee of territorial integrity' in Article 10 of the League of Nations Covenant, 'whatever reasons are given', even if the state in possession of the invaded territory lacks good title. I referred in my first lecture to the analogy drawn by Sir John between this guarantee of possession and that in Henry II's assize Novel Disseisin ('Sovereignty, Seisin and the League', *British Year Book of International Law*, 1926, p. 37). This, of course, does not mean that a state whose title to territory is explicitly recognized by international adjudication is barred from 'forcible entry' authorized by the United Nations.

[5] Article 2, paragraph 5. This differs from Article 10 of the League Covenant in that it does not create an obligation of member states to 'preserve' others against 'external aggression' but only an obligation to assist the United Nations in such action.

[6] H. Lauterpacht, *The Development of International Law by the International Court*, revised ed., London, Stevens, 1956.

order must under present conditions give priority to the state, the requirements of justice cannot ignore the individual. Ultimately, the state is for man, not man for the state. A major purpose of the United Nations is to assure the observance of human rights, the self-determination of peoples, and the economic, social, and cultural progress of all mankind. These 'purposes'[1] are intended as guides to 'international co-operation'[2] through the United Nations and the Specialized Agencies. The extent to which the Charter has implemented them by principles legally binding upon members has been controversial. National courts and the General Assembly have found positive obligations of member states in the 'pledge' of Article 56 in regard to human rights. The General Assembly has found members legally bound by the 'obligation' of Article 73 to promote the welfare and self-government of the inhabitants of non-self-governing territories. Full realization of these purposes, however, requires more specific agreements.

In this lecture I will consider only the primary function of international law. This involves consideration of the scope and structure of the society it seeks to order, and of the rules which must be observed to maintain order under present and emerging conditions of international relations.

2. THE SCOPE OF THE INTERNATIONAL JURAL ORDER

It seems clear that a jural order to afford security to states must be universal. Self-defence by national forces or collective defence by alliances have been major reliances for security in the past. The development of the latter through such collective defence organizations as NATO and Warsaw, and the close economic, social, and political relations of regional groups of states, have induced suggestions of limited international jural orders. European International Law, American International Law, Communist International Law, Moslem International Law, Free World International Law, Commonwealth International Law, etc. have been suggested, but it seems clear that the major dangers threatening the security of states are from across regional lines. Conditions of the world, discussed in my last lecture, arising from present military technology, have made it clear to both soldiers and statesmen that no state and no alliance system can gain genuine security through its internal resources or

[1] United Nations Charter, Preamble and Articles 1, 55, 73, 76.
[2] *Ibid.*, Article 1, paragraph 3; Article 56.

activities alone. Policies of active and passive defence, of massive and graduated retaliation, of stabilized deterrence and flexible response, of subsidized local forces and paramilitary operations have been adopted or proposed but have failed to create confidence that general nuclear war, if not initiated deliberately, will not be started by pre-emptive, irresponsible, or catalytic attack, or through accident, miscalculation, or the escalation of limited hostilities.

Solution of the problem by developing a universal jural order, within which mutual trust may grow and disarmament become possible, is undeniably difficult in a world with most of its military power divided into two camps, thus preventing the co-ordination of overwhelming power against aggression by one of these camps. Educators, statesmen, administrators, and lawyers must co-operate if these difficulties are to be surmounted. But no other solution promising relative stability seems likely.[1]

3. THE STRUCTURE OF A UNIVERSAL JURAL ORDER

It is difficult to envisage a form of jural order which would be both tolerable and feasible in the immediate future, except one based on the peaceful coexistence of states—that is, on mutual respect for the territorial integrity and political independence of equal sovereign states. Qualifications of sovereignty in the interest of human rights, self-determination of peoples, and social, economic, and cultural progress for all may be introduced by particular or general agreements of the states affected, or may be authorized by international procedures similarly accepted.

This is the structure upon which the international jural order has rested during the past few centuries, and it has been maintained by a military balance of power. The factors noted, militating against individual or collective defence or deterrence by military means, also militate against a stable military balance of power. This does not mean that an equilibrium of power can be wholly dispensed with. Any jural order, international or national, rests on some sort of equilibrium, but under present conditions the equilibrium must be much more complicated than a simple military confrontation, as it is in democratic, constitutional systems which balance the parts against each other and each against the whole, utilizing not only the potential power of the sword, but also the power of the purse, the power of the

[1] Wright, *The Strengthening of International Law*, The Hague, Academy of International Law, Recueil des Cours, 1959, chap. III.

word, and the power of the law. It may be noted that whenever the international balance of power has been relatively stable, it has not, in fact, been a purely military balance but a multipolar equilibrium in which diplomacy, economy, opinion, and law have played an important part.[1]

Forms of jural order proposed as alternatives to a military balance of power have been those of world empire or hegemony, world federation, and international organization.[2]

While there has been no experience of a literally universal empire, many civilizations, as Arnold Toynbee has pointed out, have moved from systems of military balance of power to universal states established by conquest and ruled from a centre controlling dominant military power. The Ts'in Empire following the period of warring states in China, the Maurya Empire after Alexander's invasion of India, the Roman Empire after Julius Caesar, the empires of Charlemagne, of the Arab Caliphates, of Genghis Khan, of Napoleon, and of the Soviets are illustrations of land empires, differing from the sea empires, after the Renaissance, of Spain, Portugal, Britain, the Netherlands, and France. All empires implied dominant military force at the centre, direct administrative authority, or indirect authority through hegemonial relationships over subject peoples. Empires, it is true, have always rested upon some sort of equilibrium —sometimes among factions at the top, sometimes among rival agencies of central power such as the army, the secret police, the party, and the administration, and sometimes between the government and subject peoples threatening revolt. The size of empires has in the past been limited by the technology of communication from the centre to the periphery. The Roman Empire depended upon Roman roads throughout Europe, and the British Empire upon a large merchant marine and predominant sea power. Such equilibria have seldom been sufficiently stable to prevent the breakdown of the structure, usually in a relatively short time. In so far as empires have developed the economy and political awareness of subject peoples, they have defeated themselves. The parts, having acquired both the will and capability of self-government, have revolted or have been granted independence, as in the more recent history of the British Empire.[3]

[1] *Ibid.*, chap. VI.
[2] I have discussed these forms of structure in *A Study of War*, Chicago, 1942, pp. 965 ff.
[3] Wright, 'Empires and World Government before 1918', *Current History*, August, 1960, pp. 65 ff.

Political theory has more commonly contemplated hegemonial relationships than equality among states, and Socialist theory, placing the rivalry of classes ahead of the rivalry of territorial states, has contemplated at least temporarily a universal dictatorship of the leaders of the proletariat, but the concept of universal empire has decreased in popularity since the rise of international law. To Dante in the fourteenth century, a universal empire seemed a natural solution for the problem of preserving peace. Few would take that position today. The dictatorship of the proletariat is not advocated as a system of universal empire even by the Communists, but as a temporary situation, ushering in the withering away of the state and a system of free co-operation in which coercion is unnecessary.

In spite of this opinion the Soviet government has had considerable success in maintaining and expanding a highly centralized system, ruling many diverse peoples, for a generation, but the restlessness of some subject areas, the differences between the great centres of Communist power in Moscow and Peking, and the general demand for greater personal liberty as living standards rise make it unlikely that the Soviet Empire will continue in its present form for a long period, even if fears of external attack continue and the inherent difficulty of succession to the central authority, always a serious problem in imperial structures, is overcome. In any case, the prospect of expansion of the Soviet system into a literal world empire seems extremely small. Even if Communism should be accepted by many underdeveloped countries in Asia, Africa, and Latin America, these are more likely to subordinate that ideology to nationalism, as Yugoslavia and China have done, than to remain willing or unwilling subjects of Moscow or Peking. Development of either Communist ideology or Soviet control in the more highly industrialized Western world is improbable, in spite of the considerable Communist parties in Italy and France and the ephemeral existence of such phenomena as the late Senator Joseph McCarthy and the John Birch Society in the United States with their obsessive fears of Communist expansion.[1]

The Security Council of the United Nations, dominated by the great powers which together control most of the world's military power, has great theoretical legal power, to be exercised with a high degree of discretion. There is, however, little prospect of the United Nations developing into a five-headed world empire, although

---

[1] It was suggested in Congress that the latter might change its name to 'sons of birch', and might adapt the slogan 'Drive dangerously—the next pedestrian you kill may be a Communist.'

during the Second World War both President Roosevelt and Prime Minister Stalin referred to their own countries and Britain as the 'policemen' of the world. In spite of the potentially centralized executive power, the United Nations has no centralized legislative power, and the prospect of agreement among the 'policemen' does not seem great. It is to be noted, however, that some of the smaller powers, remembering Munich, insisted that the Security Council must exercise its discretion with due consideration for 'justice' (Article 1, paragraph 1; Article 2, paragraph 3), 'international law' (Article 1, paragraph 1; Article 36, paragraph 3), and the domestic jurisdiction of states (Article 2, paragraph 7). Both constitutional and practical considerations offer insuperable obstacles to the United Nations developing into a world empire.[1]

We must conclude that a universal empire centralizing legal authority over both persons and nationalities is not feasible, nor is it considered desirable by peoples that have enjoyed a considerable measure of constitutional democracy, prosperity, and freedom within their nations.

Strong movements for world federation have grown up, in the West especially, as projections by Americans of their own form of government to the world. Federations of moderate dimensions existed in ancient Greece, among certain Italian and German cities in the Middle Ages, and in modern times in the United States, Switzerland, Canada, Australia, Mexico, Brazil, and modern India; but federations have been even smaller in area than empires, though longer lived. Resting on voluntary agreement rather than central force, they have been established only among peoples with considerable similarity in culture and law, and with a common interest in international co-operation and external defence.[2]

Federation implies a division of legislative authority between centre and state, subject to change only by procedures more difficult than ordinary legislation. In a strict sense it refers to organizations (Bundesstaaten) in which the central authority acts directly on

---

[1] For my opinion in 1946 that the United Nations might face the alternative of empire or federation, see my *Problems of Stability and Progress in International Relations*, University of California Press, 1954, pp. 74 ff., reprinting an article from the *Yale Law Journal*, August, 1946; and for that in 1941, calling for a more federalistic world organization than the League of Nations, see 'Peace and Political Organization', Commission to Study the Organization of Peace, *Preliminary Report*, and Monographs, *International Conciliation*, No. 369, April, 1941, pp. 457 ff., and *Fundamental Problems of International Organization*, ibid., pp. 485 ff.

[2] See p. 51, n. 3.

individuals, but is sometimes used to include confederations (Staaten-bunden) in which the central authority acts only on states as such. All types of federation differ, however, from empires, in that the component states enjoy theoretical, and usually practical, autonomy and the authority of the centre is limited by constitutional law and practical checks and balances.[1]

In spite of the persuasive arguments of world federalists, the achievement of their goal is little more likely in the foreseeable future than that of a universal Soviet empire. Throughout the Communist third of the world, the idea of world federation is no less anathema than is the idea of a universal Communist empire to the West. The uncommitted third of the world, composed in considerable measure of newly established states which generally favour national independence, regards subordination within a universal federation as a new form of imperialism. Even in the West, apart from federalistic developments in the various Western European communities, there has been no evidence of a general willingness to accept a world legislature with authority to make law applicable to individuals within the states in matters of political importance. While the United Nations Charter and proposals made in the General Assembly carry suggestions of central legislative authority to protect human rights, to punish international crimes, to inspect disarmament agreements, and to regulate areas outside of the territory of any state such as the high seas, the bed of the seas, the Antarctic, and outer space, no such authority has actually been created. The legislative authority of international organizations has been confined to regulation of their own Secretariats, determination and apportionment of budgets, and regulations supplementing conventional rules on postal, telecommunication, and other services with no great political importance.[2] Most states have even been unwilling to accept without reservations the jurisdiction of the International Court of Justice in legal disputes, a type of supernational authority to which states have in the past been less resistant than to legislative authority. It seems unlikely that the United Nations can develop into anything deserving the name of

[1] E. A. Freeman (*History of Federal Government from the Foundation of the Achaian League to the Disruption of the United States*, London, 1863) uses the term in a general sense. See also Wright, *op. cit.*, p. 50, n. 1 above, pp. 197 ff.; and p. 51, n. 2 above, pp. 776 ff., 969, 982; and p. 53, n. 1 above, final citation, pp. 485 ff.

[2] Commission to Study the Organization of Peace, 13th Report (A. N. Holcombe, ed.), *Developing the United Nations*, 1961, pp. 35 ff.; 11th Report, *Organizing Peace in the Nuclear Age*, 1959, pp. 12 ff., 33 ff.; *op. cit.*, p. 50, n. 1 above, pp. 133 ff.

world federation until commercial and cultural interchange, philosophical synthesis of divergent ideologies, and common conceptions of justice have developed and considerably augmented the solidarity of the community.

We must, therefore, conclude that while aspects of balance of power, empire, and federation are to be found in contemporary international relations and in the United Nations itself, the basic structure of the order which it is the function of international law to define, maintain, and regulate is that described in the Charter as the principle of the sovereign equality of states, each committed to respect one another's territorial integrity and political independence; each exercising domestic jurisdiction over its form of government, economy, and ideology; and each maintaining the military, executive, judicial, legislative, and administrative power essential for the support of that jurisdiction.

Such a structure, known as 'international organization', is *sui generis* manifesting more resemblance to confederation than to other historic forms of political organization. It differs from federation in its decentralization and the slight direct relation of the centre to individuals, and from hegemony in the equality and consent of member states. It remains to be seen whether this form of organization, which the historian Edward Freeman regarded as inherently unstable, can continue, avoiding the tendency which Freeman noted either to break up into sovereign nations or to unite under central government.[1]

International organization gives primary attention to territorial sovereignty, and since military attack has been the commonest method of violating territorial sovereignty, its first task, emphasized in the preamble of the United Nations Charter, has been to prevent such attack. The first task of international law should therefore be to identify sovereign states and the territory of each, to prevent military invasion, to control armed forces so as to reduce the probability of such invasions, and to limit their destructiveness if hostilities occur. The rules concerning recognition, aggression, disarmament, and military necessity are therefore the primary concern of the international order.

This materialistic analysis of the function of international law is obviously incomplete. The state's domain extends beyond territory to sea and air, and the state has interests beyond its domain in its nationals, its national ships, its diplomatic and other official agencies;

[1] See p. 54, n. 1 above.

in marine resources, and in raw materials, markets, communication, and transport facilities; and in other opportunities and advantages in the territory of other states. Even beyond this, states are interested in epidemic diseases, ideologies, and barbarous practices abroad which may infect its own population, and in expectations of co-operation, friendship, or hostility from other governments. Many of these interests which extend into the domain of other states or conflict with their interests have been regulated by customary practices or treaties creating reciprocal rights and obligations; thus from the point of view of international law, the competence of each state within that portion of space known as its domain is qualified by obligations owed to other states. Exclusive competence or domestic jurisdiction is not, therefore, a material phenomenon, measured by physical boundaries, but a legal situation determined by the state's obligations under international law.

Nor is military invasion the only way in which a state's enjoyment, control, and disposition of its domain may be imperilled. Infiltration, bribery, espionage, sabotage, assassination, guerilla activities, propaganda, threats, embargoes, discriminations, retortions, reprisals, and other activities of foreign governments and individuals may subvert governments, officials, and organizations; alienate, impoverish, or starve populations; and destroy the state's welfare, independence, and security. In the modern world, these modes of intervention may be no less dangerous than military invasion.

It follows that the armed forces or military capability at the disposal of potentially hostile governments is not the only aspect of their power which a state has to fear. Armament in being, including armies, navies, air forces, missiles, nuclear and conventional weapons, are only one aspect of military power. It includes also industrial potential, population, resources, and technology for making armaments; morale of the armed forces, government, and people for using them effectively; and reputation, prestige, and a favourable image in the minds of other governments and peoples predisposing them to be friendly or at least neutral rather than hostile. But in addition to these elements of military power, a state may exert influence over or in other states by economic, psychological, cultural, moral, or intellectual capabilities. Independence in the development of these modes of influence is, however, the essence of sovereignty. The law cannot qualify it without departing from the basic concept of international organization. It can only insist that disputes and conflicts be settled peacefully and seek to develop procedures so that they will be settled justly.

Justice, however, may mean the application of existing law, or it may mean the application of a higher law. Aristotle distinguished commutative justice, which gives to each his own as defined by law, from distributive justice, which gives to each according to his deserts as defined by the most fundamental values of the society. In well-developed societies, the first is the province of courts, the second of legislatures. But in less developed societies, the two cannot be segregated. Positive law cannot be clearly distinguished from natural law. Nevertheless, controversies concerning rights which the parties claim under law can be distinguished from those concerning interests demanded above or irrespective of law. Controversy about the latter raises the issue of peaceful change and of the legal or political principles which should guide it, such, for example, in the international community, as promotion of respect for human rights, of the self-determination of peoples, and of the social and economic welfare of mankind.

The theory of the law concerning the matters discussed in the preceding paragraphs—domestic jurisdiction, intervention, pacific settlement, and peaceful change—cannot be expressed in precise rules of order, but only in broad principles or complex rules of justice. These principles, however, cannot be realized in a jungle world. The Society of Nations is still in a situation where strict law defining the basic rules of order protecting the territory of recognized states against military attack is the first requirement. But if confidence in the basic order can be established, principles of justice, distinguishing domestic from international jurisdiction, distinguishing illegitimate intervention from legitimate influence, promoting procedures and principles for settling disputes within that order, and for developing the law itself better to realize the aspirations of men and nations, may be administered. Before considering these principles, brief attention will be given to the rules concerning recognition, aggression, arms control, and military necessity.

4. RECOGNITION

Only states, and national or international agencies upon which they have conferred that authority, are considered by international law competent to exert power in international relations. But what are states? Power, even military power, has in fact been exerted in international relations by belligerent, insurgent, and other *de facto* governments and by guerilla forces and armed bands without acknowledged authority from any *de jure* state. Confusion has arisen from the uncertainty whether a state is a phenomenon of fact or of law. Realists say a state exists whenever a government exercises independent authority over a people, living in a territory, whatever other states may think of it. *Ex factis jus oritur.* Others say that such entities are not states unless generally recognized as such by the existing members of the community of nations. They may pay respect to the *de facto* theory by asserting that when the conditions of *de facto* statehood exist, other states ought to accord recognition, but still maintain the constitutive theory, insisting that until general recognition has been accorded there is no state in international law. Still other writers, subordinating both fact and law to politics, say recognition is wholly discretionary and can properly be used as an instrument of policy to influence communities seeking recognition, and should be withheld unless the applicant state, by its declaration and its behaviour, indicates an intention and ability to observe international law or to pursue a policy favourable to the recognizing state. There are also the questions: How many recognitions constitute general recognition? and What is the relation between recognition of a state and of its government?[1]

The basic principle of international law, demanding mutual respect by each state for the sovereignty of others, requires precise determination of what are existing sovereign states. This precision might be accomplished by adopting a strict defactoism and requiring states to accept the decision of the United Nations in this matter. This would imply that only members of the United Nations have that quality, that the government whose representative is accepted by the General Assembly is the government of the state, that the United Nations should admit all *de facto* states to membership, and that the General Assembly should accept the *de facto* government of all members. A state or government should be held to exist *de facto* as soon as it manifests prospects of permanence, irrespective of its intentions, its ideology, or its acts. In deference to the Stimson doctrine and the principle *jus ex injuria non oritur*, if the state or government was established through acts clearly in violation of international

---

[1] Wright, 'Some Thoughts about Recognition', *American Journal of International Law*, July, 1950, vol. 44, pp. 548 ff.; 'Recognition, Intervention, and Ideologies', *Indian Year Book of International Affairs*, 1958, pp. 89 ff.

obligations, the United Nations might withhold recognition so long as there is a prospect of rectifying the situation.[1] However, a proper balance between facts and rights would seem to justify recognition by the United Nations of a state or government which has continued to exist in fact for a considerable period of time, irrespective of the mode of its establishment.

While there is a trend toward this position,[2] the policy of certain states (supported by Article 4 of the Charter) seeking to use non-recognition as an instrument of national policy has prevailed for over a decade. The result has been such anomalies as the non-admission of three divided states, the acceptance of the government of Formosa as the government of China, and variations in the recognition of these entities among states. The dangers in this situation become greater as time goes on.

5. Aggression

The United Nations Charter and the Kellogg-Briand Pact seek to outlaw war as a legal institution and to prevent war in the material sense by providing for a cease-fire whenever international hostilities occur; and, if this is not successful, providing for determination of the aggressor and permitting or requiring non-participating states to discriminate in their treatment of the belligerents. The traditional concept of a state of war as a situation in which the belligerents are equally entitled to settle their conflict by the use of armed force and other states are obliged to observe neutrality, cannot exist in principle.[3] The definition of aggression is clearly vital to this objective of eliminating war, both legally and materially.

The term aggression has psychological, military, political, and legal connotations inducing much confusion in its definition. The Charter, however, uses the term to refer to *illegal uses of armed force*

[1] Wright, *Legal Problems in the Far Eastern Conflict*, Institute of Pacific Relations, 1941, pp. 3, 91, 117, 134 ff., 181 ff.

[2] This position, which resembles the Estrada doctrine, is given considerable support by the late Judge Lauterpacht (p. 47, n. 2 above) and by Malbone W. Graham, *The League of Nations and the Recognition of States: In Quest of a Law of Recognition*, University of California at Los Angeles, 1933. See also Wright, 'The Chinese Recognition Problem', *American Journal of International Law*, July, 1955, vol. 49, pp. 320 ff. Though it accords with the traditional defactoism of U.S. recognition policy, the United States has in recent years been its most vigorous opponent.

[3] Wright, *A Study of War*, pp. 891 ff.

in international relations.[1] Thus Article 1 refers to the 'suppression of acts of aggression or other breaches of the peace', and Article 39 requires the Security Council to determine the 'existence of any threat to the peace, breach of the peace, or act of aggression'. This determination appears to be a sanction for the obligation of members under Article 2 'to settle their international disputes by peaceful means' and to 'refrain in their international relations from the threat or use of force'. The latter phrase seems to be equivalent to the term in Article 51 'armed attack' which justifies individual or collective self-defence. It must be assumed that 'armed attack' means only illegal armed attack. Clearly a legitimate armed attack, in defence or under the authority of the United Nations, cannot justify the original aggressor in defensive measures or permit others to help him under the head of 'collective defence'. Thus, 'breach of the peace', 'use of force', and 'armed attack' seem to be equivalent terms all referring to military action, which has been designated 'aggression' if the action is illegal and the responsible state has been identified.

It is unfortunate that differences of phraseology were used. Since a 'threat' of force is put in the same category as a 'use of force', and a 'threat to the peace' is put in the same category as a 'breach of the peace', it is not unreasonable to assume that an 'armed attack' is intended to include an immediate threat of armed attack, thus justifying military counteraction in individual or collective self-defence before there is an actual attack. This construction is, of course, in

---

[1] This meaning was implied by the Politis Report in the League of Nations Disarmament Conference on May 24, 1933, adapted in the 'Convention Defining Aggression' of July 3, 1933, which went into force between the Soviet Union and eleven surrounding states, and was referred to with approval by the Chief of the U.S. Prosecution, Mr. Justice Jackson, during the Nuremberg trial, *Record*, p. 168 (Manley O. Hudson, *International Legislation*, vol. 6, p. 410, including bibliography). It was accepted by the Harvard Research in International Law in 1939 after an exhaustive examination of treaties and diplomatic correspondence using the term (*American Journal of International Law*, 1937, Supp., pp. 827 ff., including a bibliography and the texts of over a hundred uses of the term in official documents). This meaning of the term is implied in most of the proposed definitions printed in the Appendix of Julius Stone, *Aggression and World Order*, 1958, though a few include subversive acts not involving the use of armed force. The present writer, in 1935, defined an aggressor as 'a state which may be subjected to preventive, deterrent, or remedial measures by other states because of its violation of an obligation not to resort to force' ('The Concept of Aggression in International Law', *American Journal of International Law*, July, 1935, vol. 29, p. 375, with considerable bibliography, pp. 373 ff., and 'The Prevention of Aggression', *ibid.*, July, 1956, vol. 50, p. 526). Those who find it difficult to define 'aggression' because of its psychological connotations (see Stone, p. 48, n. 4 above) might avoid this difficulty by defining the circumstances in which the use of armed force is illegal in international relations.

accord with traditional international law which recognized, as in the Caroline incident, the right of self-defence when there is an 'instant and overwhelming necessity'.[1] With this construction, however, it is clear that the 'threat' in Articles 2 and 39 implies something much more immediate than the 'danger to the maintenance of international peace and security' referred to in Articles 33 and 34, or the 'impairment of the general welfare or friendly relations among nations' referred to in Article 14. The Charter seems to recognize four stages in the process toward war in the material sense; impairment of friendly relations, danger to the maintenance of peace, threat to the peace, and actual breach of the peace or use of armed force. Military defensive measures are permissible at most only in the last two situations.

With this concept, an act of aggression can be defined as the use or threat to use armed force across an internationally recognized frontier or against armed forces of another government, for which a government *de facto* or *de jure* is responsible because of act or negligence, unless justified by a necessity for individual or collective self-defence, by the authority of the United Nations to restore international peace and security, or by consent of the state within whose territory armed force is being used.[2]

This definition seems to conform to the Charter's general prohibition of threat or use of force in international relations in Article 2, paragraph 4, subject to the qualifications made by the Charter itself in respect to defence (Article 51), to the authority of the United Nations itself (Chapter VII), and, by implication from the basic principle of sovereign equality (Article 2, paragraph 1), which permits states to make agreements for co-operation in legitimate activity. Armed intervention, however, is not permissible by invitation of either the recognized or the rebelling faction in case of civil strife. If it were, the 'right of revolution' implicit in the concepts of state sovereignty and self-determination would be denied. In a situation of civil strife, the *state* is temporarily inhibited from acting. A government beset by civil strife is not in a position to invite assistance in the name of the state.[3]

---

[1] Phrase used by Secretary of State Webster, 1842. J. B. Moore, *Digest of International Law*, vol. 2, p. 412; Wright, 'Meaning of the Pact of Paris', *American Journal of International Law*, 1933, vol. 27, p. 44; 'The Outlawry of War', *ibid.*, 1925, vol. 19, pp. 90 ff.; 'Repertory of United Nations Practice', vol. 2, pp. 432 ff., on Article 51, sec. 10.

[2] Wright, *op. cit.*, p. 50, n. 1 above, p. 162.

[3] *Ibid.*, 'United States Intervention in Lebanon', *American Journal of International Law*, January, 1959, vol. 53, pp. 112 ff.; 'International Law and Civil Strife', *Proceedings*, American Society of International Law, 1959, pp. 145 ff.

This definition of aggression was implied by the judgment of the Nuremberg Tribunal, which assumed that Hitler's invasions would be aggression unless justified by defensive necessity or invitation of the state in whose territory the force was used. These justifications were pleaded by certain defendants in respect to the invasions of Norway and Austria respectively.[1] There was, of course, no suggestion that any of Hitler's invasions were justified by international authority.

The basic concept that aggression constitutes illegal resort to armed force is implied by most of the numerous uses of the term in treaties, by most of the discussions in the League of Nations and the United Nations, and by most of the definitions which have been proposed by jurists. The Harvard Research insists that the 'resort to armed force must have been duly determined by a means which a state is bound to accept to constitute a violation of an obligation'. It is generally recognized, however, that efforts should be made to stop fighting without waiting to determine which belligerent is responsible and is therefore the aggressor. A finding that there has been a use of armed force or a breach of the peace can be, and usually has been, made in first instance, and a cease-fire, equally applicable to both belligerents, ordered by international authority. The cease-fire should, of course, order the belligerents to withdraw from any territory they may have occupied during the hostilities. This may prove difficult, as it did in Israel's invasion of Egypt in 1956. Consequently, it is important that the cease-fire be issued immediately, before there have been any such occupations.[2] This procedure is recommended by Article 40 of the Charter; and, if it is successful, there is no immediate need to determine the aggressor, although such need may arise later to decide claims to reparation, as was true in the Greco-Bulgarian incident of 1926. If one belligerent accepts the cease-fire and the other does not, the latter may be provisionally branded as the aggressor. Such provisional determination, however, is not necessarily conclusive.

According to the proposed definition, forces are considered 'used' in international relations only if they are used across 'an internationally recognized frontier or against armed forces of another state'. This distinction is clearly suggested in Article 2, paragraph 4,

[1] International Military Tribunal, Nuremberg, *Judgment*, p. 194; Wright, 'The Law of the Nuremberg Trial', *American Journal of International Law*, January, 1947, vol. 41, p. 66.
[2] Wright, 'The Concept of Aggression', p. 60, n. 1 above, pp. 389, 393.

of the Charter, which forbids 'the threat or use of force against the territorial integrity or political independence of any state, or in any other manner inconsistent with the purposes of the United Nations'. It is clearly contrary to the 'purpose' requiring 'respect for the principle of equal rights and self-determination of peoples' for a state to intervene on its own initative on behalf of either faction during civil strife in another state, even if invited to do so by the recognized government of the latter state; but a United Nations organ may declare that civil strife under particular circumstances, such as existed in the Congo in 1960, constitutes a 'threat' to international peace, and may recommend or decide upon measures to be taken by members to maintain or restore peace (Article 39). It is also contrary to the 'purpose' requiring that international disputes be settled only by peaceful means, as well as to the explicit obligation to this effect (Article 2, paragraph 3), for a state to engage in military reprisals or other form of forcible self-help to maintain rights which it claims against another state, even rights affirmed by the International Court of Justice. The Security Council may, however, 'make recommendations or decide upon measures' to be taken by members 'to give effect to such a judgment' (Article 94).

It seems clear that a state using force against another state in accord with such recommendations or decisions of a United Nations organ would not be violating Article 2, paragraph 4, because it would be acting in accord with a clearly determined 'purpose of the United Nations'. On the other hand, the basic principle of mutual respect by states for one another's equal sovereignty, territorial integrity, political independence, and domestic jurisdiction prohibits military intervention by a state on its own responsibility. Consequently, such intervention, in the absence of a necessity for self-defence or any explicit authorization by a United Nations organ within its competence, cannot be justified on the ground that it is intended to carry out one of the 'purposes' stated in the Charter (Article 1). These are 'purposes of the United Nations' and only an organ of the United Nations can determine what action is suitable to implement them in particular circumstances.

It also seems clear that no organ of the United Nations except the Court has the authority to settle international disputes or situations. The Security Council (Chapter VI) or, if it fails to function, the General Assembly (Articles 11, 12, 35) may make recommendations to the parties to facilitate a settlement, but it cannot recommend forcible measures to implement such proposals. The Charter clearly distinguishes the powers of the United Nations to maintain peace and to enforce World Court judgments from those to facilitate pacific settlement, and in respect to the latter neither the United Nations nor a state may use force.[1]

This limitation upon the authority of the political organs of the United Nations, together with the limited jurisdiction of the Court, has resulted in many unsettled disputes. The United Nations has stopped fighting in many situations—Iran, the Greek frontier, Kashmir, Indonesia, Palestine, Korea, and Suez—but in several of these (Kashmir, Palestine, Korea) a settlement has not been reached and the peace continues endangered by supposedly temporary armistice lines. The same is true in other situations which have not come directly before the United Nations (Germany, the Straits of Formosa, Vietnam, Laos). These situations are unfortunate, but they are the necessary result of the conviction of states that peace must come before justice, of their willingness to establish authority to stop fighting, but of their unwillingness to accept authoritative procedures to settle disputes except through acceptances of the jurisdiction of the International Court of Justice, which remains rather limited.

The failure of the United Nations General Assembly to define 'aggression', although the meaning seems fairly clear from the Charter itself, seems to have resulted from the desire of some states to retain the right of military reprisals to obtain what they regard as justice if peaceful methods fail, as asserted by Great Britain in the Suez incident, and of others, especially the United States, to include in the concept of aggression various forms of subversive intervention characterized as 'indirect aggression'. Either of these conceptions would seem to do away with the prime purpose of the term aggression in the Charter, to limit the use of armed force to clearly defined circumstances. Such qualifications would tend to convert the term aggression from a rule of order to a principle of justice.[2] If armed force can be used to rectify injustice, then the legitimacy of its use depends on prior determination of the merits of the dispute which has resulted in a use or threat of force. From the first discussion of the subject of aggression in the League of Nations, it has generally been recognized that elimination of the use of military force in international relations must be treated as a rule of order and separated

---

[1] Sir Frederick Eggleston in Victor H. Wallace, ed., *Paths to Peace*, Cambridge University Press, 1957, p. 325.

[2] This seems to have been the object of Julius Stone's criticism. P. 48, n. 4 above.

from the merits of international disputes. The Charter's distinction between procedures of pacific settlement (Chapter VI) and of peace maintenance (Chapter VII) indicates the same insistence. The effort to identify aggression with 'unjust war' in the medieval sense, which regarded war as just if designed to remedy injustice, is quite contrary to the conception of aggression used in League of Nations and United Nations discussions. It would mark an abandonment of the efforts to prevent hostilities by law, although that effort is certainly more necessary in the atomic age than ever before.

6. DISARMAMENT

It has been recognized that if power is available, it is likely to be used; consequently the rules of order limiting the use of force by states in international relations should be accompanied by regulations limiting the power available to them.

State power, as noted, includes arms in being, industrial potential for making arms, civilian and military morale, and reputation attractive to allies. Efforts have been made to limit all of these aspects of power by disarmament agreements but with little success. Discussion and negotiation have been devoted primarily to arms in being, with more attention to their control to maintain an equilibrium of power than to their reduction in order to augment the power of the United Nations in relation to its members, or to save money, although the latter objectives have been supported in United Nations resolutions calling for general disarmament.[1]

Limitations of industrial potential were sought in the Baruch Plan for complete international control of the atomic energy industry, and some regulation, to this end, is involved in the Atoms for Peace Agency.[2] States are, however, extremely reluctant to limit in any way their industrial development.

The control of morale, often stimulated by fear or hatred of a traditional enemy, has been attempted in efforts of UNESCO to induce states to regulate school textbooks so that they will not maintain or stimulate international feuds in the rising generation. However, the propaganda of nationalism and patriotism has been regarded as a major element of internal stability. States are, therefore,

[1] Philip Noel-Baker, *The Arms Race*, London, 1958; Wright, *A Study of War*, pp. 792 ff.
[2] Commission to Study the Organization of Peace, 11th Report: *Organizing Peace in the Nuclear Age*, A. N. Holcombe, ed., New York University Press, 1954, pp. 119 ff.

generally unwilling to contemplate regulation of their educational or propaganda activities for international purposes.[1]

Attacks on the reputation and stability of a state by hostile radio propaganda were criticized in the League of Nations Disarmament Conference, and 'moral disarmament' to prevent such attacks was proposed by a treaty on this subject which was signed and ratified by a considerable number of states in 1935.[2]

Disarmament of all kinds has, however, resulted in more talk than agreement, though some local disarmament agreements, such as that between the United States and Great Britain concerning the Great Lakes in 1817, and some limited agreements such as that made at the Washington Conference of 1922 on capital ships, have been achieved. No general rule of order on the subject has emerged. Recent disarmament discussions have centred around efforts to prevent surprise attack and nuclear testing, the major difficulty being the problem of inspection. The prevention of surprise attack is related to morale, since anxieties on this subject may have a psychological influence tending to induce pre-emptive war. The ban on nuclear testing is related to industrial disarmament since the object is to prevent the spread of nuclear weapons and industry to further countries, which would augment the dangers of accidental or irresponsible war, but in addition it has the object of preventing deleterious nuclear fallout.

It seems likely that disarmament can only be a gradual process, beginning with an improved international atmosphere won through skilful diplomacy, permitting controls to stabilize deterrence and to further a decrease in international tensions and an increase in mutual trust. This may, in turn, make possible reductions in armaments, both qualitative and quantitative. Every agreement should contribute to a relaxation of tensions and the development of an atmosphere more conducive to general disarmament, embodied in a rule of order, limiting armaments to those necessary for domestic order and international policing.[3]

---

[1] Wright, p. 50, n. 1 above, chap. II; *The Study of International Relations*, New York, 1955, pp. 318 ff.; Charles E. Merriam, *The Making of Citizens*, University of Chicago Press, 1931.

[2] Manley O. Hudson, *International Legislation*, vol. 7, p. 409; Wright, 'The Crime of "War-Mongering" ', *American Journal of International Law*, January, 1948, vol. 42, pp. 128 ff.

[3] James P. Warburg, *Disarmament, The Challenge of the Nineteen Sixties*, New York, Doubleday, 1961, pp. 150 ff.; Grenville Clark and Louis B. Sohn, *World Peace Through World Law*, Harvard University Press, 1958, Appendix I (Disarmament), pp. 203 ff.

7. MILITARY NECESSITY

So long as hostilities may occur, some limitation upon military activity has always been considered desirable to reduce its ravages. Limitations in time, in space, in tactics, and in technology to reduce losses of human life, resources, and values, to make restoration of peace less difficult, and renewal of war less likely, have been accepted in practice and conventions, in spite of the occasional inconsistency of these objectives with one another and with the objectives of the belligerents.[1]

To these ends, the rules of war have sought to reconcile these inconsistencies and limit the use of force, even when such use is permissible as was formerly the case during a legal 'state of war' and is still the case under the Charter during defensive or policing operations against aggression, or, so far as international law is concerned, during civil strife.

They do so by declaring that no use against enemy territory, forces, civilians, or others is permitted, except under 'military necessity', that is, to forward a rational strategy for defeating the enemy. Wanton destruction of life or property is, therefore, forbidden.[2] Furthermore, the rules of war specifically forbid certain acts of an unnecessarily inhumane or perfidious character. The killing of prisoners of war or of innocent civilians in occupied territory, and violations of the Red Cross emblem, flags of truce, or armistices are in this category.[3]

In situations of aggression, the aggressor in principle should gain no advantage from his unlawful hostilities. He cannot plead a military necessity for his acts destructive of life and property, and he is liable to make reparations for all such losses. The defending powers, on the other hand, enjoy normal belligerent prerogatives. Both sides, however, are bound to observe regulations of the law of war in the interests of humanity and good faith. Since the aggressor will seek

[1] Wright, *A Study of War*, pp. 155 ff., 810 ff.; 'Limited War and The United Nations', *Bulletin of the International House of Japan*, winter, 1959, pp. 1 ff.; 'The New Law of War and Neutrality', *Nederlands Tijdschrift voor Internationaal Recht*, July, 1959, vol. 6, pp. 412 ff.

[2] See IV Hague Convention, 1907; U.S. Rules of Land Warfare, Basic Field Manual, F.M. 27–10, 1940, Article 23–26.

[3] *Ibid.*, and Geneva Conventions, 1949, *American Journal of International Law*, Supp., October, 1953, pp. 119 ff. (Prisoners of War); July, 1956, pp. 729 ff. (Civilians); and Jean S. Pictet, ed., *The Geneva Conventions of August 12, 1949*, with Commentary, 4 vols., Geneva, International Committee of the Red Cross, 1956–1960.

to win the war, he will in fact act as a lawful belligerent, the legal difference being manifested in claims for reparation after the war and in differential treatment by third states during the war. Third states are bound to give no aid to the aggressor and are permitted to assist the defending state, both as a matter of principle and by explicit provision in the United Nations Charter (Article 2, paragraph 5).[1]

In addition to its general use, military necessity is used in a special sense to indicate unusual circumstances permitting the overriding of qualified restrictions in the law of war, or even, in extreme cases, in overriding explicit prohibitions in the law of war as a measure of reprisal.[2] Rules of war, which have in considerable measure been codified,[3] should be regarded as rules of order, regulating the use of force, rather than as principles of justice.

The rules of order determining states and their territory, defining and prohibiting military aggression, controlling military capability, and regulating the conduct of hostilities, are not sufficiently precise. Even if better defined and enforced, they would not produce a just world. They might, however, maintain a more peaceful and secure world order, within which principles of justice and means to assure their observance could develop.

[1] Harvard Research in International Law, *Draft Convention on Rights and Duties of States in Case of Aggression*, Philip Jessup, Reporter, Articles 2, 3, 33, *American Journal of International Law*, Supp., 1939, pp. 828, 886; Wright, *op. cit.*, p. 50, n. 1 above, pp. 152 ff.; 'The Outlawry of War and the Law of War', *ibid.*, July, 1953, vol. 47, pp. 365 ff.

[2] U.S. Rules of Land Warfare, Article 358.

[3] For texts of Declarations of Paris (1856), St. Petersburg (1868), and London (1909), and Conventions of Geneva (1864, 1868, 1906) and The Hague (1899, 1907), with commentaries, see A. Pearce Higgins, *The Hague Peace Conferences*, Cambridge University Press, 1909.

Chapter V

THE PROSPECTS OF INTERNATIONAL LAW

1. LAW AND CHANGE

INTERNATIONAL law has suffered from the criticisms that it does not reflect justice and that it is not enforced. In this lecture I will consider these two criticisms.

International law has not been a static system. Both rights under the law and rules of law themselves have often changed in response to changes in the conditions of international relations and changes in conceptions of justice. These changes, however, have not always been peaceful, have not always been well timed, and have not always been in the direction of progress. They have frequently occurred as the result of unilateral declaration, insurrection, conquest, or war, although national and collective policies of recognition, the negotiation of bilateral and general treaties, and the slow processes of acquiescence, custom, juristic analysis, and judicial precedent have also played a role. This role, however, has more often been as a confirmation than as an initiator of change.[1]

As indicated by the usual practice of recognizing *de facto* changes, the law has often been obliged to adapt itself to changing conditions. It has not often been able to change conditions so that they will better accord with the values it professes to maintain, although this has been attempted in recent times, especially in the 'Stimson doctrine', refusing recognition of fruits of aggression. Political action, initiated by states in their own interest, has been more important in modern international relations than the law of the Society of Nations as a whole. The world is, therefore, faced by the problem of achieving a better balance between law enforcement and political change.[2]

The prevalence of violent, untimely, and deteriorating change of

[1] Quincy Wright, 'Article 19 of the League of Nations Covenant', *Proceedings*, American Society of International Law, April, 1936, pp. 55 ff.

[2] Morton A. Kaplan and Nicholas de B. Katzenbach, *The Political Foundations of International Law*, New York, Wiley, 1961, pp. 4 ff.; Wright, *Legal Problems in the Far Eastern Conflict*, Institute of Pacific Relations, 1941, pp. 7 ff.; Percy Corbett, *Law in Diplomacy*, Princeton University Press, 1959, pp. 271 ff.

law and rights, and the incapacity of law to modify conditions which frustrate the realization of its values, has raised the question whether the group of coexisting nations can be regarded as a jural society, and whether the rules which those nations profess in their foreign relations can be regarded as law. Jurists have usually asserted that, as a necessary condition of the existence of international law, there is a 'Society of Nations', though sometimes they have preferred the words 'Community' or 'Family' because these words imply close contact, abundant communication, or common culture rather than social solidarity, common political goals, and accepted legal standards. However, it seems preferable to follow the scientific method when answering questions concerning the existence of phenomena which vary in time. That method assumes that answers can be only relative, and not absolute. A jural society may exist, at a given point in history and in a given locality, in greater or lesser degree. 'Sociologists have come to think of groups not as entities but as continuous processes of becoming and disappearing.'[1]

It may be said that a perfect jural society is one in which the will of the society prevails over that of its members, in which the values of the law prevail over the practices of the culture, in which deductions from abstract rules of law prevail over inferences from the concrete facts of a situation, and in which actions to realize the purposes of the law prevail over inconsistent conditions. Yet no jural society exemplifies such 'perfection', and most people would say that a society is far from perfect if it neglects individual interests in deference to the social will, if it ignores local or social customs in deference to general law, if it ignores the peculiarities of the facts of the case in deference to abstract rules, and if it ignores the conditions of life in deference to the purposes of the law. A jural society is not 'perfect' if it is so planned by law that men are sacrificed. The whole and the part, the desirable and the actual, the abstract and the concrete, the active and the established, must be kept in balance if the society is to serve man.[2]

Let us, therefore, agree that a Society of Nations exists, or has existed, although, compared with national societies, it is excessively decentralized, customary, fact-guided (*ex factis, jus oritur*), and passive. It appears, however—and this certainly was the conviction of the architects of the League of Nations and the United Nations—

---

[1] Wright, *A Study of War*, p. 1033. See also pp. 971 ff.
[2] *Ibid.*, pp. 975 ff., 1344 ff.; *Problems of Stability and Progress in International Relations*, 1954, pp. 34 ff.

that present conditions require a universal jural society which is more centralized, less customary, more able to control conditions (*ex injuria jus non oritur*), and less satisfied with its own passivity. To this end, a better balance should be sought between the rule of facts and of values,[1] by establishing rules of order to prevent violence so far as possible under existing conditions, and by declaring principles of justice to supplement traditional international law.[2] Both were to be utilized in the procedures set up by the United Nations for the peaceful settlement of disputes and situations.

Do present conditions permit international law to maintain justice by peaceful processes? Can rules of order be maintained against recalcitrant states without jeopardizing either peace or justice? These problems were raised dramatically in the events of the autumn of 1956, the first in the Suez situation, and the second in the Hungarian situation. Similar problems have been raised more recently in the Congo, Laos, and Cuba, and are threatened in Vietnam, the Straits of Formosa, and Berlin. They are, superficially, problems of international politics and organization, but, fundamentally, they are problems of international law.[3]

Everyone assumes the desirability of avoiding war, an assumption which seems obvious in an age of missiles and hydrogen bombs, but opinions on what justice requires differ greatly. The world is faced by the problem of reconciling common demands for freedom from nuclear destruction with divergent demands for freedom to promote self-determined concepts of justice and interest by self-determined methods. Solution of this problem seems to require that the basic rules of order, discussed in my last lecture, be established, and that they be supplemented by principles of justice, reconciling or accommodating the divergent values and interests of nations, and reflected in effectively maintained rules of law.

To what extent is it desirable to supplement the claim to territorial sovereignty by a claim to domestic jurisdiction; the claim to freedom from aggression by a claim to freedom from intervention of any kind; the claim to relief from threatening armaments by a claim to assurance that all disputes will be settled justly; and the claim to act

---

[1] H. Lauterpacht, *Recognition in International Law*, 1947, p. 426.

[2] National courts usually enforce foreign judgments based on general principles of justice, but not those based on particular rules of order (*ordre public*) such as penal, political, or revenue laws. Kaplan and Katzenbach, *op. cit.*, pp. 176, 181.

[3] Wright, 'Interventions, 1956', *American Journal of International Law*, April, 1957, vol. 5, pp. 257 ff.; 'Legal Aspects of the Berlin Situation', *ibid.*, October, 1961; p. 40, n. 1 above.

under military necessity by a claim to benefit by principles promoting human freedom and progress?

2. DOMESTIC JURISDICTION

States are entitled to monopolize power within their territories, and to use it at discretion to maintain their domestic jurisdiction. The latter is sometimes used as equivalent to territorial domain, but states cannot exert power over foreign embassies or foreign warships in their territory, and they can exert power over their own ships at sea, over their warships in foreign ports, and over leased foreign territory. Domestic jurisdiction cannot, therefore, be defined by geography, but only by law. It may be defined as the capacity of a state to exercise jurisdiction in any situation whatever, except in so far as it is under obligations of international law or treaty in respect to the situation.[1] Whether a proposed exercise of power is within a state's domestic jurisdiction cannot, therefore, be determined until all of its obligations bearing on the situation have been examined. For this reason, the International Court of Justice often attaches preliminary pleas of domestic jurisdiction to the merits of the dispute, and if it does make a preliminary judgment against the plea, it does so only 'provisionally'. The principle that neither a state nor an international organization can intervene in the domestic jurisdiction of a state turns out to be a principle of justice rather than a rule of order. It can be determined only after scrutiny of the merits of all the claims in a given situation.

The increasing abundance of communications, transportation, and travel across national boundaries, resulting in both widespread interdependencies and widespread vulnerabilities, have given each state very real interest in what goes on in the territory of others. From the point of view of actual interest, few questions, therefore, can be regarded as wholly domestic. If law is to reflect actual conditions, it should give protection to these actual interests. It should recognize a state's claim to reparation because of injuries to itself or its nationals resulting from events which occur within another state's territory, and should permit a state and its nationals reasonable access to trade, information, cultural exchange, and transit in the territory of other states.

[1] 'Tunis Nationality Decrees Case', Hudson, *World Court Reports*, vol. 1, p. 156; 'The Lotus', *ibid.*, vol. 2, p. 65; Wright, *The Strengthening of International Law*, p. 204.

Starting from the concept of territorial sovereignty, such rights have actually developed by custom, such as diplomatic immunity, innocent passage in the territorial sea, protection of citizens abroad, and the sharing of international rivers; and by treaties, such as those regulating trade, migration, cultural exchanges, postal and tele-communications; river, land, and air transits, and epidemiological control. The development of such rights and correlative obligations qualifying territorial sovereignty has reduced the exclusiveness of territorial jurisdiction. The domestic jurisdiction of states in the legal sense, being the residuum remaining unregulated by international law or treaty, has therefore been continually reduced as the real interest of states in the territory of others has been recognized and given legal protection. States are no longer isolated islands; each, as John Donne suggested, is part of the others. Thus, by agreement and practice, claims for justice have developed rules of law supplementing territorial sovereignty.[1]

3. INTERVENTION

A basic rule of order protects states from aggression, that is, from armed invasion, but there are many other ways in which the government of a state, or persons in its territory, may injure another state or even threaten its existence. Propaganda, espionage, infiltration, corruption, sabotage, assassination, embargo, threat, display of force, diplomatic demands and other methods may be used to stir up disorder in another state, to destroy its markets or sources of raw materials, to induce violaton of its laws, to destroy its prestige and reputation, to control its policy, or to subvert its government. Acts of this kind for which a government is responsible appear unjust and certainly deteriorate international relations. They are often grouped under the head 'intervention', a term which has eluded clear definition.[2]

Intervention has usually been defined as dictatorial interference in the internal affairs or foreign policy of a state, but the terms 'dictatorial' and 'interference' themselves require definition. Some writers have regarded intervention as a normal procedure to obtain justice.[3] Most, however, consider it in principle illegal, because manifesting a

[1] Wilfred Jenks, *The Commonwealth of Man*, London, 1958.
[2] Charles Grey Bream, *Intervention Short of Armed Force in Latin America*, abstract of dissertation, University of Chicago, 1945, p. 17. The term 'indirect aggression', sometimes used for such acts, seems inappropriate, for reasons explained in my last lecture, see p. 64 above.
[3] Ellery Stowell, *International Law*, New York, Holt, 1931, p. 72.

lack of respect for the independence of other states, though permissible in exceptional circumstances.[1] Even military interference, for defence, for assisting the United Nations in policing operations, or for assisting another state within its territory—circumstances which would save the acts from being aggression—are permitted, but are not usually called intervention. Intervention is not, however, confined to military measures. Inter-American conventions forbid it, if military or diplomatic, direct or indirect, and particularly in the case of civil strife.[2]

However, some qualifications are necessary. A diplomatic protest alleging illegal behaviour, or a representation pointing out injuries to national interests, cannot be regarded as intervention. The tone of a diplomatic communication must be peremptory and threatening to constitute 'dictatorial interference'. It is not illegal to exert influence on another government through normal diplomacy, through internal development, or through retorsionary economic measures within a state's domestic jurisdiction. Even economic or other non-military reprisals, such as the suspension of a treaty, may be permissible if peaceful means of settlement have failed and the measures are no more severe than the injury complained of. Measures of this kind, while sometimes called 'permissible intervention', are more often given a different name, such as protest, defence, representation, assistance, interposition, intercession, retorsion, reprisals, or influence, with the suggestion that if it is intervention, it is illegal.[3]

Subversive intervention refers to acts of espionage, sabotage, infiltration, bribery, paramilitary operations, assistance to guerillas, or other acts by agents of a government within another state's territory, violative of its laws and intended to subvert or control its government. Such activity in time of peace is clearly violative of international law because it encroaches upon another state's domestic jurisdiction. As such activity is usually carried on secretly, and if discovered is not acknowledged by the responsible government, the

[1] George Grafton Wilson, *Handbook of International Law*, 3rd ed., St. Paul, West, 1939, p. 58; L. Oppenheim, *International Law*, sec. 134; Charles Cheney Hyde, *International Law*, 2nd ed., Boston, Little, Brown, 1945, vol. 1, p. 245.
[2] See Conventions Habana, 1928; Buenos Aires, 1933; Montevideo, 1933; Buenos Aires, 1936; Chapultepec, 1945; Bogota, 1948; Caracas, 1954; Manley O. Hudson, *International Legislation*, vol. 4, p. 2418; vol. 6, pp. 450, 623, 628; *American Journal of International Law*, 1952, Supp., vol. 46, p. 46; *ibid.*, July, 1954, Supp., vol. 48, p. 123. See also exchange of notes between President Roosevelt and Ambassador Litvinoff on U.S. recognition of Russia, November, 1933.
[3] See Hyde, *loc. cit.*

agent is punished under the domestic law of the country and no protest is made, unless government complicity is evident because of the diplomatic character of the agent, or is acknowledged, as by President Eisenhower in the U-2 incident of May, 1960.[1] Subversive intervention may also take place by government propaganda intended to subvert another government,[2] or by government assistance to military expeditions or revolutionists, as in the Cuban incident of May, 1961.[3]

Private propaganda or subversive activity short of military expeditions or enterprises is not usually regarded as intervention if there is no government complicity. In democratic governments, such activity, unless clearly incitive to violence, is usually considered within constitutional guarantees of freedom of speech and association. Autocratic governments have often assumed that international law requires the suppression of such activity and have made some conventions among themselves to that effect. In 1936 the League of Nations initiated a convention requiring suppression of subversive radio propaganda and in 1937 one requiring suppression of acts of international terrorism. The first of these conventions was ratified by a number of states and came into force, but not the second.[4]

The line separating illegal intervention from legitimate exertions of influence by one government upon another and the line separating subversive propaganda for which the government is responsible from exercise of free speech and association by individuals, are not easy to draw. The correspondence between the United States and the Soviet Union at the time of recognition, in which each agreed not to engage in any activity designed to upset the government of the other, and the protests and explanations which followed, indicate this difficulty. The obligation of states to respect one another's territorial integrity, political independence, and domestic jurisdiction is affected by so many factors that it should be regarded as a principle of justice rather than a rule of order, thus differing from the concept of aggression. Aggression must often be determined, at least provisionally, to meet emergency conditions, without consideration of

[1] Wright, 'Legal Aspects of the U-2 Incident', *American Journal of International Law*, October, 1960, vol. 54, p. 836.

[2] *Ibid.*, 'Subversive Intervention', *American Journal of International Law*, July, 1960, vol. 54, p. 521.

[3] *Ibid.*, 'Intervention and [Cuba', *Proceedings*, American Society of International Law, April, 1961.

[4] *Ibid.*, 'The Crime of "War-Mongering" ', *American Journal of International Law*, January, 1948, vol . 42, p. 128; M. O. Hudson, *International Legislation*, vol. 7, pp. 409, 862.

the merits of the dispute which led to it. This is less true of intervention.

The United Nations is itself forbidden to intervene in matters essentially within the domestic jurisdiction of a state (Article 2, paragraph 7), but because of the extensive powers given the United Nations to make decisions or recommendations for the purpose of suppressing violence (Article 39), settling disputes (Articles 11, 36, 37), moderating dangerous conditions (Article 14), and promoting human rights, the self-determination of peoples, and the general welfare (Articles 55, 73), its action to influence states, even by dictatorial interference, is much more extensive than that permitted to states acting individually. Because of these broad competencies, Article 2, paragraph 7, actually imposes little restriction upon the organs of the United Nations. Members are obliged by the Charter to permit organs of the United Nations to exercise the powers conferred upon them; consequently, such exercise is not an encroachment on the domestic jurisdiction of the state addressed. Furthermore, the action of United Nations organs is, in most cases, limited to 'recommendation', which would not usually constitute 'intervention', although it might if in peremptory form. Members of the United Nations, acting in pursuance of such decisions or recommendations, are clearly fulfilling a 'purpose of the United Nations' (Article 3, paragraph 4) and cannot therefore be charged with illegal intervention or aggression.[1]

4. THE SETTLEMENT OF DISPUTES

When each state was a relatively isolated island, and intercourse was confined to relatively few diplomats, merchants, scholars, and clergy, disputes were infrequent and generally concerned territorial claims and alleged acts of aggression. Geography gave some protection to all states, and a great deal of protection to some.

As the capacity of states to injure each other has developed with science and technology, creating interdependencies and vulnerabilities, the interests of states have interpenetrated, disputes have become frequent, and it has become hopeless for any to gain security by isolation of itself or disarmament of its neighbours. Security has become a function, not of eliminating disputes, but of their just settlement.

[1] Wright, *International Law and the United Nations*, New York, Asia Publishing House, 1960, pp. 53 ff.

Disputes may be settled by dictation, by negotiation, by obsolescence, or by adjudication, that is, in accord with the will of one, of both, of no one, or of a third party.

Efforts of one party to dictate a settlement to another are likely to result in violence unless there is great disparity of power. Sovereign states do not readily accede to dictation, even though the mailed fist is concealed beneath a velvet glove. War has been regarded as the final court of princes—*ultima ratio regis*—but rules of order in the Charter now bar it, with the result that disputes often remain unsettled. Weak states may commit injustices which at other times the strong would have remedied by self-help; the strong, on the other hand, are less able to commit injustices against the weak. Many disputes have remained unsettled and many injustices have not been remedied. Probably, on the whole, the elimination of violent self-help has reduced injustice, and in any case it has created conditions more favourable to the organization of justice. When might cannot make right, the strong are more willing to submit to adjudication, and the weak cannot fail to realize that in the long run their security depends on the rule of law.[1]

Negotiation has been the main instrument for dealing with disputes in international relations, but it does not assure settlement. Prolonged diplomatic negotiation may result in deadlock and no agreement. While agreements freely accepted may approximate justice between the parties, injustice may result from concealed coercion, from outside pressures by interested powers, or from the sacrifice of the rights of third parties. The suggestion that a government should negotiate only from strength illustrates the prevalence of concealed coercion. It implies that coercion by the stronger is

---

[1] Most commentators have recognized that under the conditions of the modern world, as in all primitive societies, peace must come before justice. N. Politis, *La Justice internationale*, p. 253; Charles de Visscher, 'Reflections on the Present Prospect of International Adjudication', *American Journal of International Law*, July, 1956, vol. 50, p. 474; *Theory and Reality in Public International Law*, 1957, p. 328; Joseph Kunz, 'Bellum Justum and Bellum Legale', *American Journal of International Law*, July, 1951, vol. 45, p. 533; 'Sanctions in International Law', *ibid.*, April, 1960, vol. 54, p. 339. Julius Stone, *Aggression and World Order*, 1956; Sir Gerald FitzMaurice, *Modern Law Review*, 1958, vol. 19, p. 1; and Emile Giraud, *Annuaire*, Institute of International Law, 1957, vol. 1, pp. 271, 277, influenced by the Suez episode of 1956, think the outlawing of self-help has increased injustice because of the licence it gives small states. Stone argues that the Charter can be interpreted to permit self-help as a last resort, but this position has been generally refuted. See Myers McDougal and Florentino Feliciano, 'Legal Regulation of Resort to International Coercion', *Yale Law Journal*, May, 1959, vol. 68, pp. 1079 ff.; Kaplan and Katzenbach, *op. cit.*, p. 339 citing Latin American, Arab, and Polish writers 'strongly in the same sense'. See above pp. 5, 6.

anticipated. Since each cannot be stronger than the other, this idea prevents negotiation and tends to produce an arms race, likely to end in hostilities and dictation by the victor. Thus, if negotiation is to yield a just settlement, there should be equality in bargaining power. This may be achieved by general disarmament or by an effective enforcement of the rule of order preventing threat or force in international relations.

However, even with equality of bargaining power, agreement, whether by bargain, compromise, or subordination of special interests to a higher general interest, such as that of achieving settlement, may not result, and the dispute may continue to embarrass general peace and tranquillity. This may result in action by other states to expedite agreement through a tender of 'good offices', which may lead the parties to accept a 'mediator'. Groups of states, either *ad hoc*, as in the nineteenth-century Concert of Europe, or in international organizations like the United Nations, may suggest 'commissions of inquiry' or 'conciliation' to assist agreement, or may bring pressure by resolutions invoking world public opinion or implying threats of coercion. Diplomatic proposals from great powers, or from the Security Council, in which the great powers predominate, may have this implication. While ostensibly an aid to negotiation, mediation may approach intervention and dictation by the mediator, a danger which the Hague Convention on Pacific Settlement sought to prevent by emphasizing its voluntary and advisory character (Articles 4, 5, 6).

Furthermore, the anxiety of great powers to achieve a settlement may result in consultations, like that at Munich in 1938, appeasing an intransigent great power by giving it territory of a small state unable to defend itself. The insistence in the United Nations Charter that the Security Council's recommendations for settlement should be in accord with 'justice' are doubtless to prevent such appeasements. In the lingo of balance-of-power diplomacy, they were called 'compensations', illustrated by the partition of Poland in the late eighteenth century to maintain peace between Russia, Prussia, and Austria. The unwillingness of states to give organs of the United Nations more than recommendatory power in dispute settlement, thus giving each litigant a veto, is another indication of the fear of appeasement by political bodies exercising this function.[1]

Obsolescence refers to the settlement of a dispute by changed circumstances which render the claims of the disputing states un-

[1] Wright, *The Strengthening of International Law*, chap. 13.

important. This may occur when an outside state threatens both, inducing them to join hands against it and to forget their grievances against each other; or it may occur if an armistice or a cease-fire line continues for a long time and is gradually accepted as a permanent boundary in accord with the principle of prescription. Such an emollient influence of time cannot, however, be relied upon. More often, failure to agree results in action on the part of each, diplomatically or militarily, to create conditions which it hopes will be more favourable to subsequent negotiation. Unsettled disputes, such as those which divide Germany, Korea, Vietnam, Palestine, China, and Kashmir by armistice lines, are not good for peace.

In view of the uncertainty of dictation, negotiation, or obsolescence as means to settle disputes justly, or, in many cases, to settle them at all, attention has turned to adjudication. In the broader sense, adjudication refers to settlement by an outside agency competent to make a decision binding the parties. It includes arbitration, where the litigants establish a tribunal for the particular case, and judicial settlement, where they submit to an established tribunal. In international relations both types of tribunal are presumed to apply international law, but in *ad hoc* arbitration the freedom of the parties to choose the arbitrators assures considerable political flexibility, and, furthermore, the parties are competent to agree upon rules which the tribunal is bound to apply. States may also authorize a political body to settle a dispute. By a provision in the Peace Treaty of Lausanne of 1924, Turkey and Great Britain, on behalf of Iraq, submitted the Mosul boundary dispute to the League of Nations Council for final settlement. The peace treaty with Italy after World War II provided for final settlement of the status of the Italian colonies by the United Nations General Assembly. In both cases, the political body was not competent until negotiation during a prescribed period had failed to reach agreement. Such political arbitrations are not common. States, if they are willing to submit to third-party adjudication, usually prefer a tribunal bound by law, although it has been said that in the Chinese tradition, arbitration by a 'good man' was preferred. Far Eastern states, and indeed all states of non-European civilization, have been hesitant to utilize international adjudication.[1] The scepticism of the Soviet government about either

[1] Jean Escarra, *Le Régime des concessions étrangères en Chine*, The Hague, Academy of International Law, Recueil des Cours, 1929 (II); Wright, *op. cit.*, above p. 69, n. 2, pp. 8 ff.; *op. cit.*, above p. 78, n. 1, pp. 77 ff.; 'Asian Experience and International Law', *International Studies*, Indian School of International Studies, New Delhi, July, 1919, vol. 1, pp. 71 ff.

the goodness or the impartiality of any man has hitherto prevented its submission to any form of adjudication.[1]

The International Court of Justice is bound to apply law, and many states, by becoming parties to the optional clause, have accepted its jurisdiction for the settlement of all disputes of a legal nature with other parties. The abundance of reservations, especially on the part of the great powers, and the refusal by the Communist states and most of the new states of Asia and Africa to accept the optional clause at all, indicates either incomplete confidence in the Court or in the law which it applies, or perhaps a preference for political negotiation.

Human experience has shown that adjudication by an impartial tribunal, as the final resort if negotiation fails, is the method by which justice can be best administered and is, therefore, the appropriate procedure where force and dictation are outlawed. The Institute of International Law, in 1959, passed a resolution declaring:

In an international community the members of which have renounced recourse to force and undertaken by the Charter of the United Nations to settle their international disputes by peaceful means in such a manner that international peace and security, and justice, are not endangered, recourse to the International Court of Justice or to another international court or arbitral tribunal constitutes a normal method of settlement of legal disputes, as defined in Article 36, paragraph 2, of the statute of the International Court of Justice. Consequently, recourse to the International Court of Justice or to another international court or arbitral tribunal can never be regarded as an unfriendly act toward the respondent state.

The resolution went on to urge a more general acceptance by states of the clause, and elimination of destructive reservations, especially of self-judging reservations.[2]

The fact that international law recognizes that submission to adjudication is voluntary, and the refusal of many states to accept the obligation to submit, present the greatest impediment to movement by the society of nations from a primitive society, regulated mainly by rules of order against violence, to an advanced society in which there is a high expectation that controversies will be settled justly.

[1] Litvinoff wrote: 'Only an angel could be unbiased in judging Russian affairs' (L. B. Sohn, *Cases and Materials on World Law*, Brooklyn, 1956, p. 1046) and Khrushchev expressed the opinion that while nations might be impartial, individuals could not.

[2] *Annuaire*, Institute of International Law, 1959, vol. 2, p. 381.

5. PROGRESSIVE CHANGE

What is justice? Law, as I noticed in my last lecture, seeks to unite conditions and values. Its rules of order cannot depart far from the former, and its principles of justice strive to realize the latter. The task of conforming law to values is difficult in the society of nations, because of the great diversity of value systems among the nations. Comparative studies of civilizations and legal systems may, however, discover universal values and general principles of law in the spirit of the *jus naturale* and the *jus gentium* which developed primitive Roman law to a system of justice which still constitutes the basic law of much of the world. All civil-law countries have, however, found it necessary to keep this law up to date and to conform it to particular conditions by legislation. Under conditions of rapid technological and ideological change, philosophic or juristic synthesis is not enough to conform law to justice. A process of progressive change is necessary if law is to be an instrument of justice.

I prefer to speak of 'progressive' rather than 'peaceful' change, because change, even though peaceful, may be 'retrogressive'. Progressive change involves two problems: How can principles of justice be formulated to determine whether a demanded change of positive law or of territory or other legal right is in the direction of progress? What procedures might be capable of effecting desirable changes peacefully?

In addition to its rules to preserve the peace, the Charter sets forth principles of pacific settlement, of self-determination of peoples, of respect for human rights, of co-operation to advance economic and social welfare, and of effective international organization to realize these principles (Article 14). These principles are designed to guide legal change. Some of them may already constitute legal obligations for members of the United Nations (Articles 56, 73). It is clear that their realization involves a combination of political action and legal analysis.

In this work, resolutions of the General Assembly calling upon states generally to enact legislation, to make treaties, to emancipate colonies, or to redefine boundaries, thus in some cases changing their legal rights, may be of great importance. Definitions of Charter principles, as in the Universal Declaration of Human Rights, may gradually acquire legal significance, although explicitly disavowing such an intention. Perhaps more fundamental is educational work, such as that of UNESCO, creating a public consciousness of the principles of justice which should guide change if it is to mark progress rather than deterioration.

What procedures are needed to effect progressive change peacefully? Educational work and Assembly resolutions are not self-executing, important as they may be in creating a favourable atmosphere. Diplomatic discussion, both within and without the United Nations, may be useful both in creating a suitable atmosphere and in proposing specific agreements to effect desirable legal changes.

The work of the International Law Commission, designed not only to codify but also progressively to develop international law (Article 13), should be an important agency for initiating international legislation. Carefully prepared drafts are essential if international conferences are to result in general conventions which not only will develop the law in the right direction, but also will have a prospect of achieving general ratification. The work of the Geneva Conference on the Freedom of the Seas (1958), and of the Vienna Conference on Diplomatic Immunities (1961), illustrate the possibilities of this process.

The work of the Specialized Agencies can be of great importance in apprehending the changes called for by advancing technology, in creating an atmosphere of opinion conducive to change, in drafting conventions for consideration, and in initiating conferences to convert such drafts into legal commitments. The accelerating rate of technical and political change in the world, with the progress of science and the appearance of new ideologies, makes the development of these methods, combining technical knowledge and political influence, increasingly important. It is, therefore, unfortunate that the United Nations has made less use than did the League of Nations of mixed commissions, which combine in their membership individual experts appointed by international authorities and free of government instruction, with the representatives of governments. The political atmosphere promoted by ideological differences and the Soviet scepticism about individual experts, have doubtless contributed to this situation.[1]

These processes for keeping international law up to date and for progressively developing it, so that it will exemplify justice, are inadequate. It has been suggested that a more effective legislative process might be developed through concurrent action by the Assembly and the Security Council of the United Nations, at first in limited

[1] Alexander Loveday, 'An Unfortunate Decision', *International Organization*, June, 1947, vol. 1, pp. 279 ff.

fields which do not directly encroach upon the sovereignty of states, such, for example, as outer space, the bed of the sea, the high seas, and Antarctica.[1] Some of the Specialized Agencies have a limited legislative power, and General Assembly resolutions in some situations have legal effect. It is to be expected, however, that so long as states manifest reluctance to submit generally to international adjudication, they will refuse to submit to any process of international legislation in which each lacks a veto in respect to its own obligations.[2]

6. LAW ENFORCEMENT

The problem of law enforcement is not less important than that of progressive change. Stability implies reasonable capacity to predict the future, and this is not possible in a complicated society unless there is reasonable confidence that established obligations will be observed. The law, as I noticed in my first lecture, should do for man's orientation in society what science does for his orientation in the world of nature. If changing conditions are permitted to excuse violations of legal obligation beyond the restricted application of the principle *rebus sic stantibus*, the utility of law is jeopardized. The law needs to be continuously changed in a dynamic age, but it also needs to be observed.

Here, also, education plays a role. People must appreciate the importance of respect for international law. Governments must, in greater degree, identify their national interests with maintenance of that law. As Grotius said, they should appreciate that he who violates the law breaks down the bulwarks of his own security. There are, however, more tangible procedures contributing to the observance of international law.

The first forums for this purpose are the national foreign offices and national courts. The habit of reference of all foreign policy questions to the legal adviser, and insistence that the legal adviser tell the political authorities what international law requires rather than what the government, the legislature, or the public may want to hear, would encourage respect for law.[3]

[1] Commission to Study the Organization of Peace, 13th Report, *Developing the United Nations*, A. N. Holcombe, ed., January, 1961, pp. 35 ff.

[2] A. Appadori, *The Use of Force in International Relations*, Bombay, Asia Publishing House, 1958, pp. 39 ff.; Wright, *The Strengthening of International Law*, pp. 133 ff.

[3] Lord McNair's publication of the opinions of the Law Officers of the Crown indicated the degree in which this has been done in England for centuries. Most foreign offices have a legal staff.

So, also, a more extensive incorporation of international law in the national legal system, by constitutional provisions or legislative enactment, is desirable. This would give national courts authority, in the absence of explicit national legislation, or even in spite of conflicting national legislation, to apply that law in appropriate cases; or to interpret national legislation under the assumption that the legislature did not intend to violate a legal obligation. The constitutions of a number of states give direct legal effect to customary international law and treaties, and a few place this law above legislation of subordinate governmental agencies or even of the central legislative authority itself.[1]

The enforcement of international law would also be advanced by more extensive utilization of the International Court and other international tribunals. It is to be hoped that the efforts of the American Bar Association to arouse lawyers throughout the world to the importance of a world rule of law, and similar efforts of the Institute of International Law, the International Law Association, and national international-law associations, will induce more states to make declarations under the optional clause of the Court Statute, without ambiguous or destructive reservations. The principle stated in Article 36, paragraph 6, of the Statute, that the Court decides on its own jurisdiction, hardly permits states to reserve to themselves decision on the issue of 'domestic jurisdiction'. Furthermore, reservation of a right to withdraw a declaration on short notice denies the spirit of reciprocity which should exist in all declarations under the optional clause. Greater use of the advisory jurisdiction of the Court by the United Nations and other international organizations would also be helpful in developing international law, particularly in its procedural aspects.

However, the problem of enforcement of judgments of the Court will tend to increase in gravity as its compulsory jurisdiction expands. When states have voluntarily submitted a particular dispute to arbitration, they discount in advance the possibility of losing, and consequently awards have generally been carried out. When jurisdiction expands to a broad range of future legal disputes, it will more frequently happen that states will encounter an adverse judgment on a matter which they regard as of vital importance.

The major coercive authority of the United Nations is not to

---

[1] Wallace McClure, *World Legal Order*, University of North Carolina Press, 1960, pp. 192 ff.; Wright, 'Treaties as Law in National Courts', *Indiana Law Journal*, Fall, 1956, vol. 32, pp. 1 ff.

enforce international law, but to maintain peace, a more limited matter. The Charter does, however, authorize the Security Council to enforce awards of the Court (Article 94). The Council has wide discretion in the selection of means to this end and would probably prefer measures not involving direct coercion of a state. For example, it may suggest the impounding of financial assets of the delinquent state in foreign territory to pay a pecuniary award. Other methods, including the authorization of diplomatic and economic pressures, proceedings in national courts, or appeals to public opinion or to the national interest of the delinquent state, may be available. The Security Council has authority to use direct military compulsion, or to authorize its use by member states, but such a resort would seldom be expedient.[1]

It is generally recognized that the self-willed use of military reprisals by the successful state to enforce a claim, even if confirmed by a judgment of the Court, is not permitted under the Charter. It has been suggested that the elimination of such reprisals militates against the rule of law in international affairs because it makes it possible for small states—which constitute a majority of the states in the world—to refuse to submit to international jurisdiction or to carry out awards. As already noted, grave doubts can be raised against this argument.[2]

The great powers have doubtless in the past exerted compulsion upon smaller states to submit to an international jurisdiction or to accept quasi-dictation in negotiations. In so far as they are in agreement, they have maintained a certain order in the world. This order, however, has broken down when they have quarrelled among themselves and it may be doubted whether the order was ever deemed just by the smaller states which were its victims. It would appear that maintenance of the rule of order preventing the use of force or threat by any state for private purposes except necessary self-defence, would contribute to building up an international order which is both stable and just. Consequently, the development of collective security, so as to reduce the possibility of that most serious of all violations of international law, aggressive war, is of major importance from the point of view of law enforcement. So long as states are in continual fear of their lives from external attack, they will put their interest in maintaining power position

---

[1] Oscar Schachter, 'The Enforcement of International Judicial and Arbitral Decisions', *American Journal of International Law*, January, 1960, vol. 54, pp. 1 ff.

[2] Above p. 6, n. 1; p. 77.

ahead of their interest in law observance. 'Order in peace,' wrote Judge De Visscher, 'remains the fundamental need of the society of nations. Without a minimum of order, justice is powerless.' [1]

7. CONCLUSION

I conclude that if international law is to occupy a large role in human affairs, its first task is to establish rules of order to prevent war, and its second is to develop principles of international justice and procedures, both for keeping them up to date and for assuring their application in international disputes. The Charter and the Court Statute provide the framework for such a development, but the full utilization of this framework demands continuous activity on many fronts.

The Charter declares as one of its objectives 'to establish conditions under which justice and respect for the obligations arising from treaties and other sources of international law can be maintained' (Preamble). These conditions do not yet exist. To establish them involves the development of a world public opinion which synthesizes the demand for national integrity with the need for effective international co-operation. A major objective of such co-operation should be improvement of the content and observance of the rules of international law. Peoples should demand that governments identify the national interest with the progress and maintenance of international law. Progress may be measured by the degree to which principles of justice accepted in the Charter become accepted in practice. Is law moving toward the elimination of colonialism and racialism, respect for human rights, elevation of standards of living in underdeveloped areas, cultivation of a spirit of ideological tolerance and peaceful coexistence of nations, and the strengthening of collective security against aggression? While in some of these fields there has been progress, in others there has been retrogression since World War II.

The task is a large one, and for its achievement combined efforts on the educational, legal, organizational, and political fronts are necessary. Little can be expected until tensions are reduced and confidence in the world order restored. With that, stability may be reconciled with progress, nationalism with internationalism, and international law with the sovereignty of states.

[1] Charles de Visscher, *American Journal of International Law*, 1956, vol. 50, p. 574.

International law, through its rules of order, has a large role to play in the elimination of war, and, through its principles of justice, in the settlement of international disputes. Conversely, the elimination of war through diplomacy, international organization, economic assistance, and education, is of major importance in the development of international law, as is the extension of the jurisdiction of the International Court of Justice. Peace, adjudication, and law are each dependent on the others, and their reciprocal development is the way to a more satisfactory world in the atomic age.

APPENDIX 1

LEAGUE OF NATIONS COVENANT, 1920

Part I of the Treaty of Peace signed at Versailles, June 28, 1919, and of the other Peace Treaties signed in 1919 and 1920. Text published by the Secretariat of the League of Nations; it includes, in italics, amendments in force at the time of the dissolution of the League (April 19, 1946). For text of amendments which have not entered into force, see 1 Hudson, International Legislation, pp. 19–42; 8 idem, p. 152

THE HIGH CONTRACTING PARTIES,

In order to promote international co-operation and to achieve international peace and security

by the acceptance of obligations not to resort to war,
by the prescription of open, just and honourable relations between nations,
by the firm establishment of the understandings of international law as the actual rule of conduct among Governments, and
by the maintenance of justice and a scrupulous respect for all treaty obligations in the dealings of organized peoples with one another

Agree to this Covenant of the League of Nations.

Article 1

1. The original Members of the League of Nations shall be those of the Signatories which are named in the Annex to this Covenant and also such of those other States named in the Annex as shall accede without reservation to this Covenant. Such accession shall be effected by a Declaration deposited with the Secretariat within two months of the coming into force of the Covenant. Notice thereof shall be sent to all other Members of the League.

2. Any fully self-governing State, Dominion or Colony not named in the Annex may become a Member of the League if its admission is agreed to by two-thirds of the Assembly, provided that it shall give effective guarantees of its sincere intention to observe its international obligations, and shall accept such regulations as may be prescribed by the League in regard to its military, naval and air forces and armaments.

3. Any Member of the League may, after two years' notice of its intention so to do, withdraw from the League, provided that all its international obligations and all its obligations under this Covenant shall have been fulfilled at the time of its withdrawal.

APPENDIX 1

Article 2

The action of the League under this Covenant shall be effected through the instrumentality of an Assembly and of a Council, with a permanent Secretariat.

Article 3

1. The Assembly shall consist of Representatives of the Members of the League.

2. The Assembly shall meet at stated intervals and from time to time as occasion may require at the Seat of the League or at such other place as may be decided upon.

3. The Assembly may deal at its meetings with any matter within the sphere of action of the League or affecting the peace of the world.

4. At meetings of the Assembly, each Member of the League shall have one vote, and may have not more than three Representatives.

Article 4

1. The Council shall consist of Representatives of the Principal Allied and Associated Powers,[1] together with Representatives of four other Members of the League. These four Members of the League shall be selected by the Assembly from time to time in its discretion. Until the appointment of the Representatives of the four Members of the League first selected by the Assembly, Representatives of Belgium, Brazil, Spain and Greece shall be members of the Council.

2. With the approval of the majority of the Assembly, the Council may name additional Members of the League whose Representatives shall always be members of the Council; the Council with like approval may increase the number of Members of the League to be selected by the Assembly for representation on the Council.[2]

2 *bis. The Assembly shall fix by a two-thirds majority the rules dealing with the election of the non-permanent members of the Council, and particularly such regulations as relate to their term of office and the conditions of re-eligibility.*

[1] The U.S.A., the United Kingdom, France, Italy and Japan. The U.S.A. did not join the League; Italy and Japan withdrew from it in the 1930's.

[2] In virtue of this paragraph, Germany became a permanent member of the Council in 1926 and the Soviet Union in 1934, but Germany withdrew from the League in 1933 and the Soviet Union was expelled in 1939. The number of members of the Council selected by the Assembly was increased on September 25, 1922, from four to six; on September 8, 1926, from six to nine; the number was increased provisionally on October 9, 1933, to ten for the period 1933–1936; on October 3, 1936, and December 14, 1939, respectively, to eleven for the period 1936–1939, and for the period 'ending with the election of the non-permanent members of the Council in 1942'. No election took place after 1939. During its last period of existence, the Council comprised the following non-permanent members, 'elected for a term commencing immediately on their election and ending on the day of the elections held three years later': three elected in 1937—Belgium, Iran and Peru; three in 1938—the Dominican Republic, Greece and Yugoslavia; two re-elected in 1939—Bolivia and China; three elected in 1939—Union of South Africa, Egypt and Finland.

3. The Council shall meet from time to time as occasion may require, and at least once a year, at the Seat of the League, or at such other place as may be decided upon.

4. The Council may deal at its meetings with any matter within the sphere of action of the League or affecting the peace of the world.

5. Any Member of the League not represented on the Council shall be invited to send a Representative to sit as a member at any meeting of the Council during the consideration of matters specially affecting the interests of that Member of the League.

6. At meetings of the Council, each Member of the League represented on the Council shall have one vote, and may have not more than one Representative.

Article 5

1. Except where otherwise expressly provided in this Covenant or by the terms of the present Treaty, decisions at any meeting of the Assembly or of the Council shall require the agreement of all the Members of the League represented at the meeting.

2. All matters of procedure at meetings of the Assembly or of the Council, including the appointment of Committees to investigate particular matters, shall be regulated by the Assembly or by the Council and may be decided by a majority of the Members of the League represented at the meeting.

3. The first meeting of the Assembly and the first meeting of the Council shall be summoned by the President of the United States of America.

Article 6

1. The permanent Secretariat shall be established at the Seat of the League. The Secretariat shall comprise a Secretary-General and such secretaries and staff as may be required.

2. The first Secretary-General shall be the person named in the Annex; thereafter the Secretary-General shall be appointed by the Council with the approval of the majority of the Assembly.

3. The secretaries and staff of the Secretariat shall be appointed by the Secretary-General with the approval of the Council.

4. The Secretary-General shall act in that capacity at all meetings of the Assembly and of the Council.

5. *The expenses of the League shall be borne by the Members of the League in the proportion decided by the Assembly.*

Article 7

1. The Seat of the League is established at Geneva.

2. The Council may at any time decide that the Seat of the League shall be established elsewhere.

3. All positions under or in connection with the League, including the Secretariat, shall be open equally to men and women.

4. Representatives of the Members of the League and officials of the League when engaged on the business of the League shall enjoy diplomatic privileges and immunities.

5. The buildings and other property occupied by the League or its officials or by Representatives attending its meetings shall be inviolable.

Article 8

1. The Members of the League recognize that the maintenance of peace requires the reduction of national armaments to the lowest point consistent with national safety and the enforcement by common action of international obligations.

2. The Council, taking account of the geographical situation and circumstances of each State, shall formulate plans for such reduction for the consideration and action of the several Governments.

3. Such plans shall be subject to reconsideration and revision at least every ten years.

4. After these plans shall have been adopted by the several Governments, the limits of armaments therein fixed shall not be exceeded without the concurrence of the Council.

5. The Members of the League agree that the manufacture by private enterprise of munitions and implements of war is open to grave objections. The Council shall advise how the evil effects attendant upon such manufacture can be prevented, due regard being had to the necessities of those Members of the League which are not able to manufacture the munitions and implements of war necessary for their safety.

6. The Members of the League undertake to interchange full and frank information as to the scale of their armaments, their military, naval and air programmes and the condition of such of their industries as are adaptable to war-like purposes.

Article 9

A permanent Commission shall be constituted to advise the Council on the execution of the provisions of Articles 1 and 8 and on military, naval and air questions generally.

Article 10

The Members of the League undertake to respect and preserve as against external aggression the territorial integrity and existing political independence of all Members of the League. In case of any such aggression or in case of any threat or danger of such aggression the Council shall advise upon the means by which this obligation shall be fulfilled.

Article 11

1. Any war or threat of war, whether immediately affecting any of the Members of the League or not, is hereby declared a matter of concern to the whole League, and the League shall take any action that may be deemed wise and effectual to safeguard the peace of nations. In case any such emergency should arise, the Secretary-General shall on the request of any Member of the League forthwith summon a meeting of the Council.

2. It is also declared to be the friendly right of each Member of the League to bring to the attention of the Assembly or of the Council any circumstance whatever affecting international relations which threatens

to disturb international peace or the good understanding between nations upon which peace depends.

Article 12

1. The Members of the League agree that if there should arise between them any dispute likely to lead to a rupture, they will submit the matter either to arbitration or *judicial settlement* or to inquiry by the Council, and they agree in no case to resort to war until three months after the award by the arbitrators *or the judicial decision* or the report by the Council.

2. In any case under this Article the award of the arbitrators *or the judicial decision* shall be made within a reasonable time, and the report of the Council shall be made within six months after the submission of the dispute.

Article 13

1. The Members of the League agree that whenever any dispute shall arise between them which they recognize to be suitable for submission to arbitration *or judicial settlement*, and which cannot be satisfactorily settled by diplomacy, they will submit the whole subject-matter to arbitration *or judicial settlement*.

2. Disputes as to the interpretation of a treaty, as to any question of international law, as to the existence of any fact which if established would constitute a breach of any international obligation, or as to the extent and nature of the reparation to be made for any such breach, are declared to be among those which are generally suitable for submission to arbitration *or judicial settlement*.

3. *For the consideration of any such dispute, the court to which the case is referred shall be the Permanent Court of International Justice, established in accordance with Article 14, or any tribunal agreed on by the parties to the dispute or stipulated in any convention existing between them.*

4. The Members of the League agree that they will carry out in full good faith any award *or decision* that may be rendered, and that they will not resort to war against a Member of the League which complies therewith. In the event of any failure to carry out such an award *or decision*, the Council shall propose what steps should be taken to give effect thereto.

Article 14

The Council shall formulate and submit to the Members of the League for adoption plans for the establishment of a Permanent Court of International Justice. The Court shall be competent to hear and determine any dispute of an international character which the parties thereto submit to it. The Court may also give an advisory opinion upon any dispute or question referred to it by the Council or by the Assembly.

Article 15

1. If there should arise between Members of the League any dispute likely to lead to a rupture, which is not submitted to arbitration *or judicial settlement* in accordance with Article 13, the Members of the League agree that they will submit the matter to the Council. Any party to the

dispute may effect such submission by giving notice of the existence of the dispute to the Secretary-General, who will make all necessary arrangements for a full investigation and consideration thereof.

2. For this purpose the parties to the dispute will communicate to the Secretary-General, as promptly as possible, statements of their case with all the relevant facts and papers, and the Council may forthwith direct the publication thereof.

3. The Council shall endeavour to effect a settlement of the dispute, and if such efforts are successful, a statement shall be made public giving such facts and explanations regarding the dispute and the terms of settlement thereof as the Council may deem appropriate.

4. If the dispute is not thus settled, the Council either unanimously or by a majority vote shall make and publish a report containing a statement of the facts of the dispute and the recommendations which are deemed just and proper in regard thereto.

5. Any Member of the League represented on the Council may make public a statement of the facts of the dispute and of its conclusions regarding the same.

6. If a report by the Council is unanimously agreed to by the members thereof other than the Representatives of one or more of the parties to the dispute, the Members of the League agree that they will not go to war with any party to the dispute which complies with the recommendations of the report.

7. If the Council fails to reach a report which is unanimously agreed to by the members thereof, other than the Representatives of one or more of the parties to the dispute, the Members of the League reserve to themselves the right to take such action as they shall consider necessary for the maintenance of right and justice.

8. If the dispute between the parties is claimed by one of them, and is found by the Council, to arise out of a matter which by international law is solely within the domestic jurisdiction of that party, the Council shall so report, and shall make no recommendation as to its settlement.

9. The Council may in any case under this Article refer the dispute to the Assembly. The dispute shall be so referred at the request of either party to the dispute, provided that such request be made within fourteen days after the submission of the dispute to the Council.

10. In any case referred to the Assembly, all the provisions of this Article and of Article 12 relating to the action and powers of the Council shall apply to the action and powers of the Assembly, provided that a report made by the Assembly, if concurred in by the Representatives of those Members of the League represented on the Council and of a majority of the other Members of the League, exclusive in each case of the Representatives of the parties to the dispute, shall have the same force as a report by the Council concurred in by all the members thereof other than the Representatives of one or more of the parties to the dispute.

Article 16

1. Should any Member of the League resort to war in disregard of its covenants under Articles 12, 13 or 15, it shall *ipso facto* be deemed to have

committed an act of war against all other Members of the League, which hereby undertake immediately to subject it to the severance of all trade or financial relations, the prohibition of all intercourse between their nationals and the nationals of the covenant-breaking State, and the prevention of all financial, commercial or personal intercourse between the nationals of the covenant-breaking State and the nationals of any other State, whether a Member of the League or not.

2. It shall be the duty of the Council in such case to recommend to the several Governments concerned what effective military, naval or air force the Members of the League shall severally contribute to the armed forces to be used to protect the covenants of the League.

3. The Members of the League agree, further, that they will mutually support one another in the financial and economic measures which are taken under this Article, in order to minimize the loss and inconvenience resulting from the above measures, and that they will mutually support one another in resisting any special measures aimed at one of their number by the covenant-breaking State, and that they will take the necessary steps to afford passage through their territory to the forces of any of the Members of the League which are co-operating to protect the covenants of the League.

4. Any Member of the League which has violated any covenant of the League may be declared to be no longer a Member of the League by a vote of the Council concurred in by the Representatives of all the other Members of the League represented thereon.

Article 17

1. In the event of a dispute between a Member of the League and a State which is not a member of the League, or between States not members of the League, the State or States not members of the League shall be invited to accept the obligations of membership in the League for the purposes of such dispute, upon such conditions as the Council may deem just. If such invitation is accepted, the provisions of Articles 12 to 16 inclusive shall be applied with such modifications as may be deemed necessary by the Council.

2. Upon such invitation being given the Council shall immediately institute an inquiry into the circumstances of the dispute and recommend such action as may seem best and most effectual in the circumstances.

3. If a State so invited shall refuse to accept the obligations of membership in the League for the purposes of such dispute, and shall resort to war against a Member of the League, the provisions of Article 16 shall be applicable as against the State taking such action.

4. If both parties to the dispute when so invited refuse to accept the obligations of membership in the League for the purposes of such dispute, the Council may take such measures and make such recommendations as will prevent hostilities and will result in the settlement of the dispute.

Article 18

Every treaty or international engagement entered into hereafter by any Member of the League shall be forthwith registered with the Secretariat and shall as soon as possible be published by it. No such treaty or international engagement shall be binding until so registered.

Article 19

The Assembly may from time to time advise the reconsideration by Members of the League of treaties which have become inapplicable and the consideration of international conditions whose continuance might endanger the peace of the world.

Article 20

1. The Members of the League severally agree that this Covenant is accepted as abrogating all obligations or understandings *inter se* which are inconsistent with the terms thereof, and solemnly undertake that they will not hereafter enter into any engagements inconsistent with the terms thereof.

2. In case any Member of the League shall, before becoming a Member of the League, have undertaken any obligations inconsistent with the terms of this Covenant, it shall be the duty of such Member to take immediate steps to procure its release from such obligations.

Article 21

Nothing in this Covenant shall be deemed to affect the validity of international engagements, such as treaties of arbitration or regional understandings like the Monroe doctrine, for securing the maintenance of peace.

Article 22

1. To those colonies and territories which as a consequence of the late war have ceased to be under the sovereignty of the States which formerly governed them and which are inhabited by peoples not yet able to stand by themselves under the strenuous conditions of the modern world, there should be applied the principle that the well-being and development of such peoples form a sacred trust of civilization and that securities for the performance of this trust should be embodied in this Covenant.

2. The best method of giving practical effect to this principle is that the tutelage of such peoples should be entrusted to advanced nations who by reason of their resources, their experience or their geographical position can best undertake this responsibility, and who are willing to accept it, and that this tutelage should be exercised by them as Mandatories on behalf of the League.

3. The character of the mandate must differ according to the stage of the development of the people, the geographical situation of the territory, its economic conditions and other similar circumstances.

4. Certain communities formerly belonging to the Turkish Empire have reached a stage of development where their existence as independent nations can be provisionally recognized subject to the rendering of administrative advice and assistance by a Mandatory until such time as they are able to stand alone. The wishes of these communities must be a principal consideration in the selection of the Mandatory.

5. Other peoples, especially those of Central Africa, are at such a stage that the Mandatory must be responsible for the administration of the territory under conditions which will guarantee freedom of conscience and religion, subject only to the maintenance of public order and morals, the prohibition of abuses such as the slave trade, the arms traffic and the liquor traffic, and the prevention of the establishment of fortifications or military and naval bases and of military training of the natives for other than police purposes and the defence of territory, and will also secure equal opportunities for the trade and commerce of other Members of the League.

6. There are territories, such as South West Africa and certain of the South Pacific Islands, which, owing to the sparseness of their population, or their small size, or their remoteness from the centres of civilization, or their geographical contiguity to the territory of the Mandatory, and other circumstances, can be best administered under the laws of the Mandatory as integral portions of its territory, subject to the safeguards above mentioned in the interests of the indigenous population.

7. In every case of mandate, the Mandatory shall render to the Council an annual report in reference to the territory committed to its charge.

8. The degree of authority, control, or administration to be exercised by the Mandatory shall, if not previously agreed upon by the Members of the League, be explicitly defined in each case by the Council.

9. A permanent Commission shall be constituted to receive and examine the annual reports of the Mandatories and to advise the Council on all matters relating to the observance of the mandates.

Article 23

Subject to and in accordance with the provisions of international conventions existing or hereafter to be agreed upon, the Members of the League:

(a) will endeavour to secure and maintain fair and humane conditions of labour for men, women, and children, both in their own countries and in all countries to which their commercial and industrial relations extend, and for that purpose will establish and maintain the necessary international organizations;

(b) undertake to secure just treatment of the native inhabitants of territories under their control;

(c) will entrust the League with the general supervision over the execution of agreements with regard to the traffic in women and children, and the traffic in opium and other dangerous drugs;

(d) will entrust the League with the general supervision of the trade in arms and ammunition with the countries in which the control of this traffic is necessary in the common interest;

(e) will make provision to secure and maintain freedom of communications and of transit and equitable treatment for the commerce of all Members of the League. In this connection, the special necessities of the regions devastated during the war of 1914–1918 shall be borne in mind;

(f) will endeavour to take steps in matters of international concern for the prevention and control of disease.

APPENDIX 1

Article 24

1. There shall be placed under the direction of the League all international bureaux already established by general treaties if the parties to such treaties consent. All such international bureaux and all commissions for the regulation of matters of international interest hereafter constituted shall be placed under the direction of the League.

2. In all matters of international interest which are regulated by general conventions but which are not placed under the control of international bureaux or commissions, the Secretariat of the League shall, subject to the consent of the Council and if desired by the parties, collect and distribute all relevant information and shall render any other assistance which may be necessary or desirable.

3. The Council may include as part of the expenses of the Secretariat the expenses of any bureau or commission which is placed under the direction of the League.

Article 25

The Members of the League agree to encourage and promote the establishment and co-operation of duly authorized voluntary national Red Cross organizations having as purposes the improvement of health, the prevention of disease and the mitigation of suffering throughout the world.

Article 26

1. Amendments to this Covenant will take effect when ratified by the Members of the League whose Representatives compose the Council and by a majority of the Members of the League whose Representatives compose the Assembly.

2. No such amendment shall bind any Member of the League which signifies its dissent therefrom, but in that case it shall cease to be a Member of the League.

ANNEX

I. Original Members of the League of Nations Signatories of the Treaty of Peace[1]

United States of America	China
Belgium	Cuba
Bolivia	Ecuador
Brazil	France
British Empire	Greece
Canada	Guatemala
Australia	Haiti
South Africa	Hedjaz
New Zealand	Honduras
India	Italy

[1] Of these states, the United States of America and the Hedjaz did not become members of the League.

97

Japan	Portugal
Liberia	Roumania
Nicaragua	Serb-Croat-Slovene State
Panama	Siam
Peru	Czecho-Slovakia
Poland	Uruguay

States invited to accede to the Covenant[1]

Argentine Republic	Persia
Chile	Salvador
Colombia	Spain
Denmark	Sweden
Netherlands	Switzerland
Norway	Venezuela
Paraguay	

II. First Secretary-General of the League of Nations
The Honourable Sir James Eric DRUMMOND, K.C.M.G., C.B.

[1] All of these states acceded to the Covenant and the following were subsequently admitted to the League: Afghanistan, Albania, Austria, Bulgaria, Costa Rica, Dominican Republic, Egypt, Estonia, Ethiopia, Finland, Germany, Hungary, Iraq, Ireland, Latvia, Lithuania, Luxembourg, Mexico, Turkey, U.S.S.R. A total of 63 states were at one time members of the League, but 19 had withdrawn before termination of the League's activities on April 18, 1946. See Hans Aufricht, *Guide to League of Nations Publications*, Columbia U.P., New York, 1951, pp. 505 ff.

PROTOCOL FOR THE PACIFIC SETTLEMENT OF INTERNATIONAL DISPUTES; RESOLUTION, LEAGUE OF NATIONS ASSEMBLY, 1924

Article 10

Every State which resorts to war in violation of the undertakings contained in the Covenant or in the present Protocol is an aggressor. Violation of the rules laid down for a demilitarized zone shall be held equivalent to resort to war.

In the event of hostilities having broken out, any State shall be presumed to be an aggressor, unless a decision of the Council, which must be taken unanimously, shall otherwise declare:

1. If it has refused to submit the dispute to the procedure of pacific settlement provided by Articles 13 and 15 of the Covenant as amplified by the present Protocol, or to comply with a judicial sentence or arbitral award or with a unanimous recommendation of the Council, or has disregarded a unanimous report of the Council, a judicial sentence or an arbitral award recognizing that the dispute between it and the other belligerent State arises out of a matter which by international law is solely within the domestic jurisdiction of the latter State; nevertheless, in the last case the State shall only be presumed to be an aggressor if it has not previously submitted the question to the Council or the Assembly, in accordance with Article 11 of the Covenant.

2. If it has violated provisional measures enjoined by the Council for the period while the proceedings are in progress as contemplated by Article 7 of the present Protocol.

Apart from the cases dealt with in paragraphs 1 and 2 of the present Article, if the Council does not at once succeed in determining the aggressor, it shall be bound to enjoin upon the belligerents an armistice, and shall fix the terms, acting, if need be, by a two-thirds majority and shall supervise its execution.

Any belligerent which has refused to accept the armistice or has violated its terms shall be deemed an aggressor.

The Council shall call upon the signatory States to apply forthwith against the aggressor the sanctions provided by Article 11 of the present Protocol, and any signatory State thus called upon shall thereupon be entitled to exercise the rights of a belligerent.

TREATY FOR THE RENUNCIATION OF WAR (KELLOGG-BRIAND PACT), 1928

Article 1

The High Contracting Parties solemnly declare in the names of their respective peoples that they condemn recourse to war for the solution of international controversies, and renounce it as an instrument of national policy in their relations with one another.

Article 2

The High Contracting Parties agree that the settlement or solution of all disputes or conflicts of whatever nature or of whatever origin they may be, which may arise among them, shall never be sought except by pacific means.

Article 3

The present Treaty shall be ratified by the High Contracting Parties named in the Preamble in accordance with their respective constitutional requirements, and shall take effect as between them as soon as all their several instruments of ratification shall have been deposited at Washington.

This Treaty shall, when it has come into effect as prescribed in the preceding paragraph, remain open as long as may be necessary for adherence by all the other Powers of the world. Every instrument evidencing the adherence of a Power shall be deposited at Washington and the Treaty shall immediately upon such deposit become effective as between the Power thus adhering and the other Powers parties hereto.

It shall be the duty of the Government of the United States to furnish each Government named in the Preamble and every Government subsequently adhering to this Treaty with a certified copy of the Treaty and of every instrument of ratification or adherence. It shall also be the duty of the Government of the United States telegraphically to notify such Governments immediately upon the deposit with it of each instrument of ratification or adherence.

In faith whereof the respective Plenipotentiaries have signed this Treaty in the French and English languages both texts having equal force, and hereunto affix their seals.

Done at Paris, the twenty-seventh day of August in the year one thousand nine hundred and twenty-eight.

APPENDIX 4

CONVENTION FOR DEFINITION OF AGGRESSION (SOVIET UNION AND NEIGHBOURS), 1933

Article 2

Accordingly, the aggressor in an international conflict shall, subject to the agreements in force between the parties to the dispute, be considered to be that State which is the first to commit any of the following actions:

(1) Declaration of war upon another State;

(2) Invasion by its armed forces, with or without a declaration of war, of the territory of another State;

(3) Attack by its land, naval or air forces, with or without a declaration of war, on the territory, vessels or aircraft of another State;

(4) Naval blockade of the coasts or ports of another State;

(5) Provision of support to armed bands formed in its territory which have invaded the territory of another State, or refusal, notwithstanding the request of the invaded State, to take, in its own territory, all the measures in its power to deprive those bands of all assistance or protection.

APPENDIX 5

DRAFT CONVENTION ON RIGHTS AND DUTIES OF STATES IN CASE OF AGGRESSION
(HARVARD RESEARCH IN INTERNATIONAL LAW) 1939

[*The considerations of the Draft Convention on Rights and Duties of States in Case of Aggression revealed fundamental differences of opinion regarding the general organization of the draft, its underlying theories, and a number of the specific rules and principles set forth therein. The Research nevertheless presents it, without any implication that the Draft as published reflects even a consensus of the members of the Advisory Committee, hoping that its debates upon the problem may be continued among scholars throughout the world with a view to the further clarification of the subject.*][1]

INTRODUCTORY ARTICLE

The HIGH CONTRACTING PARTIES agree to be bound, as between themselves and in all situations in which the aggressor is a party to this Convention, by the following provisions relating to the rights and duties of States in case of aggression. To the end that the application of these provisions may become universally accepted as a part of the law of nations, they invite all other States to adhere thereto.

PART I—USE OF TERMS

Article 1

As the terms are used in this Convention:

(*a*) A 'State' is a member of the community of nations.

(*b*) A State's 'territory' comprises its land and territorial waters, and the air space above them.

(*c*) 'Aggression' is a resort to armed force by a State when such resort has been duly determined, by a means which that State is bound to accept, to constitute a violation of an obligation.

(*d*) An 'aggressor' is a State which has committed an aggression.

(*e*) A 'defending State' is a State which is the victim or object of aggression.

(*f*) A 'co-defending State' is a State which assists a defending State with armed force.

[1] 'The proposals contained in the Drafts, and the statements in the Comments, are not to be taken to represent the individual views of any of the persons who have taken part in their preparation.

'The Research is wholly unofficial, and the Drafts must not be taken as in any way representing the views of the Government of the United States.'

American Journal of International Law (1939), Supplement, p. 10.

(*g*) A 'supporting State' is a State which assists a defending State without armed force.

(*h*) 'Vessel' includes aircraft.

(*i*) 'Arms, ammunition and implements of war' are those articles listed in Annex I to the Draft Convention on the Rights and Duties of Neutral States in Naval and Aërial War.[1]

PART II—AGGRESSORS

Article 2

By becoming an aggressor, a State does not acquire rights or relieve itself of duties.

Article 3

(1) Subject to Article 14, an aggressor does not have any of the rights which it would have if it were a belligerent. Titles to property are not affected by an aggressor's purported exercise of such rights.

(2) An aggressor has the duties which it would have if it were a belligerent.

Article 4

(1) An aggressor does not have any of the rights which would accrue to a State not an aggressor as the result of its use of armed force.

(2) Situations created by an aggressor's use of armed force do not change sovereignty or other legal rights over territory.

(3) A treaty brought about by an aggressor's use of armed force is voidable.

Article 5

By becoming an aggressor, a State loses the right to require other States to perform the obligations of executory treaties, but is not relieved of the duty to perform the obligations of such treaties; executed treaties are not affected.

PART III—DEFENDING AND CO-DEFENDING STATES

Article 6

Against the aggressor, a State by becoming a defending State or a co-defending State, acquires the rights which, if it were a belligerent, it would have against an opposing belligerent.

Article 7

Against States other than the aggressor, a State by becoming a defending State or a co-defending State, acquires the right to take in its own territory, or on the high seas or in the territory of the aggressor, measures to cut off

[1] *Ibid.*, pp. 794–796.

the commercial or financial relations of the aggressor with other States, subject to the following rules:

(*a*) It shall not discriminate in favour of its own nationals or property or in favour of the nationals or property of any other State.

(*b*) The manner in which it carries out such measures shall be limited by the rules on visit, search, capture and adjudication which would be applicable if it were a belligerent.

(*c*) It may sequester seized or captured property but may not condemn it unless:

   (i) it is a vessel entitled to fly the flag of an aggressor; or

  (ii) it is arms, ammunition or implements of war destined directly or indirectly to an aggressor; or

 (iii) it is a vessel more than half of whose cargo by value, weight, bulk or freight, is composed of arms, ammunition or implements of war destined directly or indirectly to an aggressor.

(*d*) It may pre-empt sequestered property on payment of the fair market value.

(*e*) It shall not subject persons to treatment more severe than would be justified by the rules governing belligerent rights and duties in relation to neutrals.

Article 8

A defending State or a co-defending State may take or send seized or captured vessels or cargoes to a port of its own or of any defending State, co-defending State or supporting State.

Article 9

A State assumes the status of a co-defending State by giving notice of that fact to all other States.

PART IV—SUPPORTING STATES

Article 10

By becoming a supporting State, a State acquires the right to discriminate against the aggressor, but it may not do any act to the detriment of States other than the aggressor unless such act would be lawful if done by a defending or co-defending State. Against an aggressor, a supporting State has the rights which, if it were neutral, it would have against a belligerent.

Article 11

A State assumes the status of a supporting State by giving notice of that fact to all other States.

PART V—OTHER STATES

Article 12

A State which is not an aggressor, a defending State, a co-defending State, or a supporting State, does not, in its relations with the aggressor, have the duties which, if it were neutral, it would have to a belligerent, but, against the aggressor, it has the rights which, if it were a neutral, it would have against a belligerent.

Article 13

Subject to the provisions of Articles 7 and 8, a State which is not an aggressor, a defending State, a co-defending State, or a supporting State, has, in its relations with a defending State, a co-defending State or a supporting State, the duties which, if it were neutral, it would have to a belligerent; and has against those States the rights which, if it were a neutral, it would have against a belligerent.

PART VI—GENERAL

Article 14

Nothing in this Convention shall be deemed to excuse any State for a violation of the humanitarian rules concerning the conduct of hostilities, prescribed by international law or by a treaty to which it is a party.

Article 15

Nothing in this Convention shall be deemed to entitle any State to deprive an aggressor of territory, or to impair the political independence of an aggressor, as a penalty for the aggression.

Article 16

The HIGH CONTRACTING PARTIES shall consult together to determine the time when the foregoing articles shall cease to operate with reference to the aggression which brought them into operation.

APPENDIX 6

CHARTER OF THE UNITED NATIONS, 1945
(PREAMBLE AND CHAPTER I)

Signed at San Francisco, June 26, 1945. Entered into force on
October 24, 1945.
U.S. Department of State, Facsimile of the Charter of the
United Nations (U.S., D.S., Pub. 2368), pp. 1–20.

WE THE PEOPLES OF THE UNITED NATIONS
DETERMINED

to save succeeding generations from the scourge of war, which twice in our lifetime has brought untold sorrow to mankind, and

to reaffirm faith in fundamental human rights, in the dignity and worth of the human person, in the equal rights of men and women and of nations large and small, and

to establish conditions under which justice and respect for the obligations arising from treaties and other sources of international law can be maintained, and

to promote social progress and better standards of life in larger freedom,

AND FOR THESE ENDS

to practise tolerance and live together in peace with one another as good neighbours, and

to unite our strength to maintain international peace and security, and

to ensure, by the acceptance of principles and the institution of methods, that armed force shall not be used, save in the common interest, and

to employ international machinery for the promotion of the economic and social advancement of all peoples,

HAVE RESOLVED TO COMBINE OUR EFFORTS TO ACCOMPLISH THESE AIMS.

Accordingly, our respective Governments, through representatives assembled in the city of San Francisco, who have exhibited their full powers found to be in good and due form, have agreed to the present Charter of the United Nations and do hereby establish an international organization to be known as the United Nations.

APPENDIX 6

CHAPTER I. PURPOSES AND PRINCIPLES

Article 1

The Purposes of the United Nations are:

1. To maintain international peace and security, and to that end: to take effective collective measures for the prevention and removal of threats to the peace, and for the suppression of acts of aggression or other breaches of the peace, and to bring about by peaceful means, and in conformity with the principles of justice and international law, adjustment or settlement of international disputes or situations which might lead to a breach of the peace;

2. To develop friendly relations among nations based on respect for the principle of equal rights and self-determination of peoples, and to take other appropriate measures to strengthen universal peace;

3. To achieve international co-operation in solving international problems of an economic, social, cultural, or humanitarian character, and in promoting and encouraging respect for human rights and for fundamental freedoms for all without distinction as to race, sex, language, or religion; and

4. To be a centre for harmonizing the actions of nations in the attainment of these common ends.

Article 2

The Organization and its Members, in pursuit of the Purposes stated in Article 1, shall act in accordance with the following Principles.

1. The Organization is based on the principle of the sovereign equality of all its Members.

2. All Members, in order to ensure to all of them the rights and benefits resulting from membership, shall fulfil in good faith the obligations assumed by them in accordance with the present Charter.

3. All Members shall settle their international disputes by peaceful means in such a manner that international peace and security, and justice, are not endangered.

4. All Members shall refrain in their international relations from the threat or use of force against the territorial integrity or political independence of any state, or in any other manner inconsistent with the Purposes of the United Nations.

5. All Members shall give the United Nations every assistance in any action it takes in accordance with the present Charter, and shall refrain from giving assistance to any state against which the United Nations is taking preventive or enforcement action.

6. The Organization shall ensure that states which are not Members of the United Nations act in accordance with these Principles so far as may be necessary for the maintenance of international peace and security.

7. Nothing contained in the present Charter shall authorize the United Nations to intervene in matters which are essentially within the domestic jurisdiction of any state or shall require the Members to submit such matters to settlement under the present Charter; but this principle shall not prejudice the application of enforcement measures under Chapter VII.

APPENDIX 7

CHARTER OF THE NUREMBERG TRIBUNAL, 1945

(JURISDICTION AND GENERAL PRINCIPLES)

Article 1

In pursuance of the Agreement signed on the 8th August, 1945, by the Government of the United Kingdom of Great Britain and Northern Ireland, the Government of the United States of America, the Provisional Government of the French Republic and the Government of the Union of Soviet Socialist Republics, there shall be established an International Military Tribunal (hereinafter called 'the Tribunal') for the just and prompt trial and punishment of the major war criminals of the European Axis.

JURISDICTION AND GENERAL PRINCIPLES
Article 6

The Tribunal established by the Agreement referred to in Article 1 hereof for the trial and punishment of the major war criminals of the European Axis countries shall have the power to try and punish persons who, acting in the interests of the European Axis countries, whether as individuals or as members of organizations, committed any of the following crimes.

The following acts, or any of them, are crimes coming within the jurisdiction of the Tribunal for which there shall be individual responsibility:

(a) *Crimes against peace:* namely, planning, preparation, initiation or waging of a war of aggression, or a war in violation of international treaties, agreements or assurances, or participation in a common plan or conspiracy for the accomplishment of any of the foregoing;

(b) *War crimes:* namely, violations of the laws or customs of war. Such violations shall include, but not be limited to, murder, ill-treatment or deportation to slave labour or for any other purpose of civilian population of or in occupied territory, murder or ill-treatment of prisoners of war or persons on the seas, killing of hostages, plunder of public or private property, wanton destruction of cities, towns or villages, or devastation not justified by military necessity.

(c) *Crimes against humanity:* namely, murder, extermination, enslavement, deportation, and other inhuman acts committed against any civilian population, before or during the war; or persecutions on political, racial or religious grounds in execution of or in connection with any crime within the jurisdiction of the Tribunal, whether or not in violation of the domestic law of the country where perpetrated.

Leaders, organizers, instigators and accomplices participating in the formulation or execution of a common plan or conspiracy to commit any of the foregoing crimes are responsible for all acts performed by any persons in execution of such plan.

Article 7

The official position of defendants, whether as Heads of State or responsible officials in Government Departments, shall not be considered as freeing them from responsibility or mitigating punishment.

Article 8

The fact that the Defendant acted pursuant to order of his Government or of a superior shall not free him from responsibility, but may be considered in mitigation of punishment if the Tribunal determines that justice so requires.

Article 9

At the trial of any individual member of any group or organization the Tribunal may declare (in connection with any act of which the individual may be convicted) that the group or organization of which the individual was a member was a criminal organization.

After receipt of the Indictment the Tribunal shall give such notice as it thinks fit that the prosecution intends to ask the Tribunal to make such declaration and any member of the organization will be entitled to apply to the Tribunal for leave to be heard by the Tribunal upon the question of the criminal character of the organization. The Tribunal shall have power to allow or reject the application. If the application is allowed, the Tribunal may direct in what manner the applicants shall be represented and heard.

Article 10

In cases where a group or organization is declared criminal by the Tribunal, the competent national authority of any Signatory shall have the right to bring individuals to trial for membership therein before national, military or occupation courts. In any such case the criminal nature of the group or organization is considered proved and shall not be questioned.

Article 11

Any person convicted by the Tribunal may be charged before a national, military or occupation court, referred to in Article 10 of this Charter, with a crime other than of membership in a criminal group or organization and such court may, after convicting him, impose upon him punishment independent of and additional to the punishment imposed by the Tribunal for participation in the criminal activities of such group or organization.

Article 12

The Tribunal shall have the right to take proceedings against a person charged with crimes set out in Article 6 of this Charter in his absence, if he has not been found or if the Tribunal for any reason, finds it necessary, in the interests of justice, to conduct the hearing in his absence.

Article 13

The Tribunal shall draw up rules for its procedure. These rules shall not be inconsistent with the provisions of this Charter.

Appendix 8

UNITING FOR PEACE
(U.N. GENERAL ASSEMBLY RESOLUTION), 1950

Resolution 377A (V) of the General Assembly, November 3, 1950. G.A.O.R., V, Supp. 20 (A/1775), pp. 10–12. With respect to questions which have arisen in connection with this Resolution, see Sohn, U.N. Law, pp. 229–247

The General Assembly,

Recognizing that the first two stated Purposes of the United Nations are:

'To maintain international peace and security, and to that end: to take effective collective measures for the prevention and removal of threats to the peace, and for the suppression of acts of aggression or other breaches of the peace, and to bring about by peaceful means, and in conformity with the principles of justice and international law, adjustment or settlement of international disputes or situations which might lead to a breach of the peace,' and

'To develop friendly relations among nations based on respect for the principle of equal rights and self-determination of peoples, and to take other appropriate measures to strengthen universal peace',

Reaffirming that it remains the primary duty of all Members of the United Nations, when involved in an international dispute, to seek settlement of such a dispute by peaceful means through the procedures laid down in Chapter VI of the Charter, and recalling the successful achievements of the United Nations in this regard on a number of previous occasions,

Finding that international tension exists on a dangerous scale,

Recalling its resolution 290 (IV) entitled 'Essentials of Peace', which states that disregard of the Principles of the Charter of the United Nations is primarily responsible for the continuance of international tension, and desiring to contribute further to the objectives of that resolution,

Reaffirming the importance of the exercise by the Security Council of its primary responsibility for the maintenance of international peace and security, and the duty of the permanent members to seek unanimity and to exercise restraint in the use of the veto,

Reaffirming that the initiative in negotiating the agreements for armed forces provided for in Article 43 of the Charter belongs to the Security

111

Council, and desiring to ensure that, pending the conclusion of such agreements, the United Nations has at its disposal means for maintaining international peace and security,

Conscious that failure of the Security Council to discharge its responsibilities on behalf of all the Member States, particularly those responsibilities referred to in the two preceding paragraphs, does not relieve Member States of their obligations or the United Nations of its responsibility under the Charter to maintain international peace and security,

Recognizing in particular that such failure does not deprive the General Assembly of its rights or relieve it of its responsibilities under the Charter in regard to the maintenance of international peace and security,

Recognizing that discharge by the General Assembly of its responsibilities in these respects calls for possibilities of observation which would ascertain the facts and expose aggressors; for the existence of armed forces which could be used collectively; and for the possibility of timely recommendation by the General Assembly to Members of the United Nations for collective action which, to be effective, should be prompt,

A

1. Resolved that if the Security Council, because of lack of unanimity of the permanent members, fails to exercise its primary responsibility for the maintenance of international peace and security in any case where there appears to be a threat to the peace, breach of the peace or act of aggression, the General Assembly shall consider the matter immediately with a view to making appropriate recommendations to Members for collective measures, including in the case of a breach of the peace or act of aggression the use of armed force when necessary, to maintain or restore international peace and security. If not in session at the time, the General Assembly may meet in an emergency special session within twenty-four hours of the request therefor. Such emergency special session shall be called if requested by the Security Council on the vote of any seven members, or by a majority of the Members of the United Nations;

2. Adopts for this purpose the amendments to its rules of procedure set forth in the annex to this resolution;

B

3. Establishes a Peace Observation Commission, which for the calendar years 1951 and 1952 shall be composed of fourteen Members, namely: China, Colombia, Czechoslovakia, France, India, Iraq, Israel, New Zealand, Pakistan, Sweden, the Union of Soviet Socialist Republics, the United Kingdom of Great Britain and Northern Ireland, the United States of America and Uruguay, and which could observe and report on the situation in any area where there exists international tension the continuance of which is likely to endanger the maintenance of international peace and security. Upon the invitation or with the consent of the State into whose territory the Commission would go, the General Assembly, or the Interim Committee when the Assembly is not in session, may utilize the Commission if the Security Council is not exercising the functions

assigned to it by the Charter with respect to the matter in question. Decisions to utilize the Commission shall be made on the affirmative vote of two-thirds of the members present and voting. The Security Council may also utilize the Commission in accordance with its authority under the Charter;

4. Decides that the Commission shall have authority in its discretion to appoint sub-commissions and to utilize the services of observers to assist it in the performance of its functions;

5. Recommends to all governments and authorities that they co-operate with the Commission and assist it in the performance of its functions;

6. Requests the Secretary-General to provide the necessary staff and facilities, utilizing, where directed by the Commission, the United Nations Panel of Field Observers envisaged in resolution 297 B (IV);

C

7. Invites each Member of the United Nations to survey its resources in order to determine the nature and scope of the assistance it may be in a position to render in support of any recommendations of the Security Council or of the General Assembly for the restoration of international peace and security;

8. Recommends to the Members of the United Nations that each Member maintain within its national armed forces elements so trained, organized and equipped that they could promptly be made available, in accordance with its constitutional processes, for service as a United Nations unit or units, upon recommendation by the Security Council or General Assembly, without prejudice to the use of such elements in exercise of the right of individual or collective self-defence recognized in Article 51 of the Charter;

9. Invites the Members of the United Nations to inform the Collective Measures Committee provided for in paragraph 11 as soon as possible of the measures taken in implementation of the preceding paragraph;

10. Requests the Secretary-General to appoint, with the approval of the Committee provided for in paragraph 11, a panel of military experts who could be made available, on request, to Member States wishing to obtain technical advice regarding the organization, training, and equipment for prompt service as United Nations units of the elements referred to in paragraph 8;

D

11. Establishes a Collective Measures Committee consisting of fourteen Members, namely; Australia, Belgium, Brazil, Burma, Canada, Egypt, France, Mexico, Philippines, Turkey, the United Kingdom of Great Britain and Northern Ireland, the United States of America, Venezuela and Yugoslavia, and directs the Committee, in consultation with the Secretary-General and with such Member States as the Committee finds appropriate, to study and make a report to the Security Council and the General Assembly, not later than September 1, 1951, on methods, including those of section C of the present resolution, which might be used to maintain and strengthen international peace and security in accordance

with the Purposes and Principles of the Charter, taking account of collective self-defence and regional arrangements (Articles 51 and 52 of the Charter);

12. Recommends to all Member States that they co-operate with the Committee and assist it in the performance of its functions;

13. Requests the Secretary-General to furnish the staff and facilities necessary for the effective accomplishment of the purposes set forth in sections C and D of the present resolution;

E

14. Is fully conscious that, in adopting the proposals set forth above, enduring peace will not be secured solely by collective security arrangements against breaches of international peace and acts of aggression, but that a genuine and lasting peace depends also upon the observance of all the Principles and Purposes established in the Charter of the United Nations, upon the implementation of the resolutions of the Security Council, the General Assembly and other principal organs of the United Nations intended to achieve the maintenance of international peace and security, and especially upon respect for and observance of human rights and fundamental freedoms for all and on the establishment and maintenance of conditions of economic and social well-being in all countries; and accordingly

15. Urges Member States to respect fully, and to intensify, joint action, in co-operation with the United Nations, to develop and stimulate universal respect for and observance of human rights and fundamental freedoms, and to intensify individual and collective efforts to achieve conditions of economic stability and social progress, particularly through the development of under-developed countries and areas.

ANNEX

[For the amended text of the rules of procedure of the General Assembly see Rules 8(b), 9(b), 10, 16, 19 and 65.]

APPENDIX 9

DEFINITIONS OF AGGRESSION PROPOSED IN U.N. SPECIAL COMMITTEE, 1956 (PROPOSAL BY THE SOVIET UNION)[1]

Paragraph 2

That State shall be declared to have committed an act of indirect aggression which:

(a) Encourages subversive activity against another State (acts of terrorism, diversionary acts, etc.);

(b) Promotes the fomenting of civil war within another State;

(c) Promotes an internal upheaval in another State or a change of policy in favour of the aggressor.

Paragraph 3

That State shall be declared to have committed an act of economic aggression which first commits one of the following acts:

(a) Takes against another State measures of economic pressure violating its sovereignty and economic independence and threatening the bases of its economic life;

(b) Takes against another State measures preventing it from exploiting or nationalizing its own natural riches;

(c) Subjects another State to an economic blockade.

Paragraph 4

That State shall be declared to have committed an act of ideological aggression which:

(a) Encourages war propaganda;

(b) Encourages propaganda in favour of using atomic, bacterial, chemical and other weapons of mass destruction;

(c) Promotes the propagation of fascist-nazi views, of racial and national exclusiveness, and of hatred and contempt for other peoples.

---

[1] *Gen. Ass. Off. Rec.*, 12th Sess. Supp. No. 16, (A/3574), p. 30. Paragraph 1 reproduces substantially the text on p. 101 above, but uses the word 'attacker' instead of 'aggressor' and inserts an additional paragraph between the third and fourth as follows: 'The landing or leading of its land, sea or air forces inside the boundaries of another state without the permission of the government of the latter, or the violation of the conditions of such permission, particularly as regards the length of their stay or the extent of the area in which they may stay.' This text also stated that other acts, declared aggression by the Security Council in a particular case, shall be considered aggression, and listed circumstances which cannot be used as justifications for acts defined as aggression.

INDEX

action, systems of, 9
adjudication, 2, 79-80
aggression, 27-8, 42, 62-5; definition of, 14, 59-60, 101, 102, 115; indirect, 64, 73n.; and intervention, 75; prevention of, 4
'Alabama' claims, 23
Albania, 16
American Bar Association, 84
'American Century', 36
Anglo-Saxon kingdoms, 3
appeasement, 78
Arab empire, 51
arbitration, 11, 13, 79
Aristotle, 57
arms, control of, 38-9
Atoms for Peace Agency, 65
Augustine, St., 19
Australia, 53
Ayala, 21

Baruch plan, 65
Belgium, 23
Bentham, Jeremy, 25
Berlin, 71
blocs, power, 29, 38; decentralization of, 42
Brazil, 53
Briand, Aristide, 5
British Empire, 51
Bynkershoek, 21, 22

Canada, 53
Catholic Church, and war, 19
cease-fire, 62
change: institutional, 7; in international law, 69; progressive, 81 ff.
Charlemagne, empire of, 51
China, 11, 24, 41, 42, 51, 52
Christendom, medieval, 19, 21
Civil War, American, 24
civilization, differences in, 11
codes, early, 1
coexistence, peaceful, 41, 42
commissions, mixed, 82
common law, 3
Communism, 39-41, 52

confederation, 55
Congo, 39, 63, 71
Connally reservation, 12
contract, social, 10
Corbett, Percy, 33
Corfu Channel case, 16
Cruce, Emeric, 25
Crusades, 19, 20
Cuba, 14, 71, 75
Curia Regis, 3

Dante, 22, 52
democracy, and law, 40
De Visscher, Charles, 5, 34, 36, 86
dictation, 77
diplomacy, and intervention, 74
Diplomatic Immunities, Vienna Conference on, 82
disarmament, 42, 43, 65-6; nuclear, 66
disputes, settlement of, 76-80
Donne, John, 73

Edward I, 3
Edward II, 4
Egypt, 62
Eisenhower, D. D., 75
empire, world, 51
empires, land and sea, 51
enforcement, of law, 83-7
England, development of law in, 3-4
entry, forcible, 48
equilibrium: imperial, 51; of power, 50
Ethelbert, Code of, 1
extraterritoriality, 24

facts, and law, 45
federation, world, 53-4
force: justice and, 2; use of, and international law, 6n.; see also aggression
foreign offices, and law, 83
Formosa, 39, 42, 59, 64, 71
Francis of Victoria, 20
Freedom of the Seas, Geneva Conference on, 82
Freeman, Edward, 55

116